The Home Buyer's Checklist

Other McGraw-Hill Books by Robert Irwin

The Home Buyer's Checklist

Robert Irwin

McGraw-Hill

New York   Chicago   San Francisco   Lisbon   London   Madrid   Mexico City
Milan   New Delhi   San Juan   Seoul   Singapore   Sydney   Toronto

Library of Congress Cataloging-in-Publication Data

The home buyer's checklist
p. cm.
ISBN 0-07-137380-2
2001042580

McGraw-Hill

A Division of The McGraw·Hill Companies

1 2 3 4 5 6 7 8 9 0 DOC/DOC 0 9 8 7 6 5 4 3 2 1

ISBN 0-07-137380-2

This book was set in Palatino by North Market Street Graphics.

Printed and bound by R. R. Donnelley & Sons Company.

McGraw-Hill books are available at special quantity discounts to use as premiums and sales
promotions, or for use in corporate training programs. For more information, please write to the
Director of Special Sales, Professional Publishing, McGraw-Hill, Two Penn Plaza, New York, NY
10121-2298. Or contact your local bookstore.

*This book contains the author's opinions. Some material in this book may be affected by changes in market
conditions or real estate law (or changes in interpretations of the law) since the manuscript was prepared.
The accuracy and completeness of the information contained in this book cannot be guaranteed. Neither the
author nor the publisher is engaged in rendering investment, legal, tax, architectural, or other professional
services. If these services are required, the reader should obtain them from a competent professional.*

This book is printed on recycled, acid-free paper containing a minimum of 50% recycled,
de-inked fiber.

Contents

CHAPTER TWO: Exterior   68

CHAPTER THREE: The Foundation   103

Introduction

Getting Started: Protect Yourself When Buying a Home

Have you ever walked through a home that was offered for sale and wondered what you should be looking at? What questions should you be asking yourself? The seller? The agent?

What should you be doing to determine if the home is in good shape or bad? If it's up-to-date or obsolete? If it has serious or modest defects? If it's a good choice in the neighborhood, or a bad one? In short, if it will make a good investment, or a poor one for you and your family?

Agents, who see hundreds of homes on a regular basis, can help. But sometimes they don't know what to look for, either. And, do you really want to rely entirely on the agent? Wouldn't you rather know what to look for yourself?

Wouldn't it be terrific if you had the experience and knowledge to know exactly what questions to ask about every detail of a "for sale" home? If you could go down a list and check off the many items you needed to know about?

That's what this book offers you. It's a personal checklist of everything you should ask when you're looking to buy a home. It covers all aspects of the property, from the neighborhood to the front driveway to the heating system to the kitchen to the backyard. It instantly converts you from a first-time "know-nothing" looker to a savvy buyer. It even suggests questions that you may want to ask your agent or the seller as you examine a property.

Use this checklist book as a guide, and it won't lead you astray. It will help you see the "for sale" home in its true light. It will keep you from overpaying and will lead you to make an educated choice and purchase a home you can be confident about.

How to Use This Book

Take it with you when you look at a home you're considering. If you're concerned about the appearance of the kitchen, check out the questions (and answers) on kitchens. If you're wondering about a door not closing, check the sections on doors. If your concern is ragged-looking carpeting or poor landscaping or any aspect of the property, check out the related questions (and answers).

Of course, you probably know that in many states sellers must give home buyers a list of disclosures detailing defects in the property. Further, buyers can demand to have the home professionally inspected. Doesn't this combination protect you when you buy?

It helps. But remember, the inspection and the disclosures normally take place *after* you've already made your purchase offer and had it accepted. At that point, if anything really bad is revealed, it's now a matter of trying to fix the deal, or get out of it . . . not deciding to get into it.

Take this checklist book with you when you first go through a property—*before* you make your purchase offer. After all, why go through the hassle of making an offer and getting it accepted, if you're not really going to want to buy the home anyway? Why pay the cost (it's the buyer who pays for the professional inspection) if you could have eliminated the home from consideration by checking it out yourself? With this book you can confidently precheck out a "for sale" property prior to making an offer to buy.

This is not to say you shouldn't carefully consider both the seller's disclosures and the professional inspection report. Indeed, if your state doesn't automatically demand disclosures of the seller, you should demand them as part of your offer. And you'll want to be sure your demand allows you time to approve or disapprove of the disclosures (usually within a few days) and the inspection report (usually within a few weeks).

However, sellers don't always disclose everything. Indeed there may be problems with the home that they are completely unaware of . . . unless and until you ask them, from questions drawn out of this book.

And professional inspectors can't see everything in an inspection that lasts just a couple of hours. However, if you've already identified several suspicious areas, you can ask the inspector to specifically check them out. The inspector can then either confirm your worst fears, or allay them. (This book, however, is not designed to take the place of a professional home inspection nor to allow you to troubleshoot problem areas.)

Finally, there's the matter of what to do if you discover a problem. Solutions are suggested thoughout the book. And if you do decide to go forward with the purchase after your checklist evaluation, you may want to insist (in the purchase offer) that the seller pay for correcting the problem, or put into writing his or her explanation. Of course, if the problem is really bad, you may want to simply walk away from the home!

Check It Out

Don't feel like and don't be a helpless buyer. Take charge of your home search. Check out each and every property you look at. Perhaps you'll want to ask only a couple of pertinent questions. Or maybe you'll have hundreds!

This book will transform you from a wide-eyed beginner to a street-wise pro. Let it protect you when you make your all-important home purchase decision.

1
Interior

Windows, Doors, and Door Frames

WINDOWS—QUESTIONS TO ASK YOURSELF

Do All Windows Open and Close Properly? ☐ yes ☐ no

In older homes, the windows sometimes jam. This is true for wood, metal, or vinyl and is caused by warping and deterioration over time. A little bath soap rubbed on areas that scrape can help temporarily, as can replacing worn rollers, if any. But often, the only long-term solution is to install new windows. See Windows below.

Is There Any Broken Window Hardware? ☐ yes ☐ no

Sometimes it can be more expensive to fix the hardware than the glass. Usually the hardware itself isn't costly, but getting the old out and the new in can be. Again, make sure the seller takes care of this.

Are Windows within 5 Feet of Shower or Bath Made of Safety Glass?   ☐ yes   ☐ no

This is a safety necessity. Safety glass will shatter in many small pieces (or will not shatter at all if it's glue laminated). Regular glass will break into large shards, which can be extremely dangerous, particularly in a bathroom. There will be a label on safety glass, usually in a corner. If it's not safety glass, it must be replaced, and it's very expensive, typically several hundred dollars per window. You'll have to negotiate this with the seller.

Are There Any Water Stains around Windows?   ☐ yes   ☐ no

Water stains suggest leaks. There may be leaks because the windows don't fit well. Or water may be coming in around the outside edges of the windows, suggesting improper installation. Get a glass contractor to look at the stains and give you an estimate on costs to fix the problem. Have the seller pay for it.

Is There Any Black Mold around Windows?   ☐ yes   ☐ no

In some areas of the country black mold is a serious problem. It rots out plaster, wood, and even gets into furnishings! If any black mold is detected, get an estimate from an exterminator. It could cost thousands of dollars to have it removed if it's in the walls.

Are There Any "Soft" Sills?   ☐ yes   ☐ no

Sometimes a wooden windowsill, or the casing, will appear soft to the touch. This suggests rotting underneath. Have an inspector check it out, usually by digging a screwdriver in to see how significant the damage is. All soft casings must be replaced. More serious can be the other unseen damage caused by leaking water.

WINDOWS—QUESTIONS TO ASK SELLER-AGENT

Do Any Windows Need Upgrading?

☐ yes   ☐ no

You may need to upgrade to double-pane, low-e, and better-quality windows. Get an estimate of the cost. Determine if it's worth it given the overall price and quality of the home. See if you can get a price reduction because of the existing poor windows.

Are Any Windows Not Working Properly?

☐ yes   ☐ no

Sometimes homes have "trick" windows that don't stay up, don't stay closed, or otherwise don't function as they should. Sometimes these are just nuisances that can be ignored. On the other hand, if the trick window is in the master bedroom or the family room, you may want to insist that the seller correct the problem.

DOORS AND DOOR FRAMES—QUESTIONS TO ASK YOURSELF

Are All Doors Leading to Garage or Exterior Solid Core?

☐ yes   ☐ no

Test by lightly tapping on the door. If there's a hollow sound, the core of the door is empty—air. You should hear a solid thump. Solid core doors provide both fire safety (it takes a long time to burn through them) and security (they are very difficult to break down). Insist that the seller provide solid core doors to all external entrances.

Do All Doors Close Properly?

☐ **yes**   ☐ **no**

Close and open each door as you go through the home. If a door doesn't work properly, note it so it can later be professionally inspected. Sometimes a door problem is simply a matter of the home shifting over time and a rehanging can solve the problem. Other times it can indicate a more serious problem with the foundation.

Do Any Doors Have Holes?

☐ **yes**   ☐ **no**

Most interior doors are hollow core. When they get a hole in them (as from a fist or other object banging through), they must be replaced. Usually they cannot be fixed. The cost is about $50 and up. Have the seller do it.

Are All Doors Well Painted or Stained?

☐ **yes**   ☐ **no**

It's usually quite easy and inexpensive to repaint a door. However, if a stained door shows marks or scratches, restaining can be more difficult and costly.

Does All the Hardware Work?

☐ **yes**   ☐ **no**

Both handles and locks (if any) should operate easily. Replacement hardware for interior doors usually costs around $25 per set.

Are There Any Missing Doors or Hardware?

☐ yes ☐ no

Sometimes sellers have removed door handles or entire doors, particularly from closets in bedrooms that were converted to offices. Determine if the removed doors and hardware are still available and in good shape. In an older house it can be nearly impossible to match old doors and hardware when you try to replace them.

Do All Doors Have Stoppers?

☐ yes ☐ no

Stoppers keep the door from banging into the wall behind it and creating a hole. A stopper only costs around a dollar, but hiring someone to patch the hole so it looks good can cost $25 and up.

Are There Any Missing Door Frame Pieces?

☐ yes ☐ no

These are sometimes removed to accommodate furniture or wall hangings. Finding replacements that match in an older home can be difficult. Ask if the original missing pieces are still available and in good shape (not broken or cracked).

Do All Hinges Work Properly?

☐ yes ☐ no

Hinges are usually brass or steel. Steel hinges can rust (leaving orange marks) and can "freeze" up. All hinges can squeak, which can usually be fixed with a tiny amount of a dry lubricant. Check to see that the screws that hold the hinges are in place. Empty screw holes usually indicate that the screw thread in the wood has been ruined. A handyperson can fix this, but it will cost a few dollars. Hinges that simply don't work or that squeak badly may indicate a warped or damaged structure or foundation—have them thoroughly inspected.

DOORS AND DOOR FRAMES—QUESTIONS TO ASK SELLER-AGENT

Are There Any Doors That Do Not Work?

☐ yes   ☐ no

You may not catch all the problems yourself. Ask to see any doors that are not working and try to determine what the problem is.

Have Any Doors Been Replaced Recently? Why?

☐ yes   ☐ no

Normally, doors in a home are never replaced, unless they are upgraded, or they have deteriorated for some reason. If the cause is deterioration, ask what was the problem? Has it been corrected so the new door will not be affected?

Wood Flooring

QUESTIONS TO ASK YOURSELF

Is It Hardwood?

☐ yes   ☐ no

Hardwood floors can be finely sanded and usually have a very smooth finish. They are considered the best wood floors. Tap on the floor with a heavy pen. You should hear a dull, thick sound.

Is It Synthetic?

☐ yes ☐ no

There are many synthetic floors; Pergo is probably the best known. Synthetic floors are usually compressed wood with a wood grain pattern printed onto a plastic-type surface. They are less expensive than hard- or softwood floors, but are more difficult to clean. Tap on the floor with a heavy pen. You should hear a hollow, reverberating sound because the floor is not actually affixed to the underlayment but floats on it.

Is It Softwood?

☐ yes ☐ no

Some older homes have pine or other softwood floors. Typically these floors have a rough surface because they do not hold a fine, smooth finish. To maintain their appearance, they usually must be resanded and restained every five to ten years. Older floors may not have enough thickness left to be resanded. Check with a flooring contractor.

Is It Scratched?

☐ yes ☐ no

Wood floors must be kept well polished to avoid scratching. Scratching usually occurs when heavy furniture is dragged across wood floors. Sometimes small scratches can be filled in and restained inexpensively. Refinishing an entire floor can cost upward of several dollars or more a square foot.

Are the Wood Floors in Potentially Wet Areas?

☐ yes ☐ no

Wood floors are great in bedrooms and living areas. They are not wonderful in kitchens, bathrooms, and laundries. Water spills can get between the wood planks and warp them, ruining the floors.

Is the Floor Warped?

☐ yes   ☐ no

You'll know if the wood floor is warped because the corners of the planks will curve up and can be felt underfoot. In very mild cases, sanding and restaining will solve the problem. In moderate to severe cases, the wood must be replaced. A new wood floor can easily cost $10 to $30 a square foot, installed.

Are Any Nails Popping Up?

☐ yes   ☐ no

Normally, wood floors are toenailed at their edges so the nails never show. In some older floors, particularly in softwood, they are nailed straight down and then the holes are filled. These nails may pop up over time. Renailing and filling is expert work and is usually done on a per-hour basis.

QUESTIONS TO ASK SELLER-AGENT

When Was the Floor Installed?

☐ yes   ☐ no

Don't assume the wood flooring came with the house, new. It may have been installed later. If it was installed less than five years ago, ask what the warranty is and if it's transferable to a new buyer.

When Was the Last Time the Floor Was Refinished?

☐ yes   ☐ no

If the seller has refinished it, ask why? Also, ask what the refinishers said was the remaining thickness of the wood. Just as with brake drums and rotors, wood floors can only be refinished a certain number of times before the boards are too thin to sand. Is there enough left for you to refinish again in the future?

What Type of Polish Do You Use?

☐ yes   ☐ no

Each type of floor requires its own type of polish. Finding out what the seller uses can save you a lot of trial and error later on.

Have There Been Any Problems with Termites Coming Through?

☐ yes   ☐ no

Homes in most areas harbor termites and these sometimes will infest flooring. Occasionally they may break through. This usually requires complete replacement of the flooring, at least in the room affected. Check the termite report and pay special attention to the findings.

Tile and Masonry Flooring

QUESTIONS TO ASK YOURSELF

How Much of the House Has Tile or Masonry?

☐ yes   ☐ no

Typically it will only be found in the entranceway, baths, and kitchen. This type of flooring is expensive, so having it elsewhere can be a plus. However, keep in mind that in most living areas, you will need to buy carpeting to cover it.

Is the Flooring Nonslip?

☐ yes ☐ no

Glazed tile can be very slippery when wet; hence, it may be a poor choice for a kitchen, baths, and utility rooms. However, it can be made slip-resistant by having small pieces of sand embedded during the glazing process. Many stones, bricks, and slates are porous, and hence are nonslip. Covering these types of flooring with carpeting will reduce the slip potential, but will also cover up the flooring.

Are There Any Missing Pieces?

☐ yes ☐ no

Rarely will tiles or other masonry pieces be missing in the middle of the floor. But sometimes end or edged pieces may be gone. Sometimes extending the connecting flooring can cover up the missing spaces. Get a flooring expert to help you with this. The cost could be anywhere from $50 to $500 or more.

Are There Any Cracked Pieces?

☐ yes ☐ no

A more common situation is cracked tiles. The only way to fix this problem is to replace the tile. However, it may be impossible to find matching tiles, particularly if they are more than five years old. Ask the seller if he or she has any extra tiles (they often do). Otherwise, plan on retiling the entire room where the cracks appear. Figure on spending $2000 to start and, depending on the quality of the tile, a lot more.

Is the Grout Discolored?

☐ yes ☐ no

White grout and other light-colored grouts are a big problem when they are discolored. You can tell by comparing the color of the grout in the walkways of the room with the grout at the edges. Two different shades indicate discoloration. This can be corrected by having about ⅛ of an inch of the grout removed and then having the tile regrouted. This will cost a minimum of $300 per room.

Does the Flooring Require Surfacing?

☐ yes ☐ no

Some brick and stone surfaces are so porous that they require surfacing about once a year, typically with a silicone sealant of some sort. (These are readily available in hardware stores.) Usually the surface must be cleaned first. It's something to consider, because you'll have to do it.

Is the Flooring Functionally Obsolete?

☐ yes ☐ no

Just because you've got a tile floor doesn't mean you've got a valuable asset to your home. If the tile is an out-of-style color or pattern, it could date the home. In this case the flooring could actually reduce the value of the property! Be sure to take this into consideration when making your purchase offer.

QUESTIONS TO ASK SELLER-AGENT

Is Any Flooring Broken or Damaged? ☐ yes ☐ no

It's unlikely you will have looked into every nook and cranny of the floor, particularly if some of it was covered with carpeting. Ask the seller to show you any broken or damaged tiles, stones, bricks, and so on. Then you can evaluate if there is a serious problem.

Has Any Flooring Been Replaced Recently? Why? ☐ yes ☐ no

If the seller recently replaced the flooring, ask why. Was there a water problem? Was it corrected? Who did the work? Was it a professional, or was it the seller? A badly done application might need to be redone within just a few years.

Are There Any "Lifting" Problems? ☐ yes ☐ no

This is hard to spot unless you walk over every tile on the floor. Ask the seller if any tiles are lifting up, where they are located, and why he or she hasn't corrected the problem. (You can tell if tiles are not securely fastened because they will make a hollow sound when tapped with a sharp object, such as a screwdriver—don't tap too hard or you'll break them!) Usually the problem is water underneath or a shifting floor, which suggests a much bigger problem. Have it thoroughly inspected by a professional inspector.

Vinyl Flooring

QUESTIONS TO ASK YOURSELF

Where Is the Vinyl Flooring Located?   ☐ yes   ☐ no

Because of its ability to resist moisture, vinyl flooring is best placed in
kitchens, baths, washrooms, and basements. Although excellent quality
vinyls, linoleums, and similar types of flooring are now available, they
are sometimes considered less desirable than wood or tile. As a consequence, homes with vinyl flooring are sometimes perceived as being of
lesser quality.

Does It Have Scratches?   ☐ yes   ☐ no

All types of vinyl flooring will have scratches. Some types, however,
are amazingly resistant. When the surface is torn and scratches appear,
there is little that can be done to fix them, short of replacing the flooring. A typical vinyl floor in a kitchen can easily cost $500 to $1000 or
more to replace, depending on quality.

Are There Any Tears?   ☐ yes   ☐ no

These are usually found at the edges of solid piece flooring. Tears can
occur when the flooring is not properly glued to its base, or where there
is an inappropriate base. Sometimes water will get under the tile (as
when it seeps up through a cement floor that has not been properly
sealed). Usually full replacement is the remedy. Regluing the torn portion may leave an ugly scar.

Is the Flooring Coved?   ☐ **yes**   ☐ **no**

Linoleum and vinyls are sometimes curved up a short distance (around 3 inches) to the surrounding walls. This makes them easier to clean. The process has become less fashionable of late, although it remains more expensive to do. Cracks or tears in the coving require replacement of the entire floor.

If Tiles, Are the Connecting Edges Clean or Dirty?   ☐ **yes**   ☐ **no**

Vinyl squares are commonly sold in hardware and home improvement stores and are easy to lay down because they are usually self-adhesive. However, the adhesive will often seep up at the edges after a short time of wear and will attract dirt. Dirt can also get into the cracks between vinyl squares. This is nearly impossible to clean, and the best treatment is to replace the flooring. Vinyl squares vary enormously in price from less than a dollar a square to well over $5 a square.

Is the Flooring Functionally Obsolete?   ☐ **yes**   ☐ **no**

Even if the flooring is in good shape, the color or pattern may be old-fashioned. This will date the house and make the entire property less valuable. Consider this when making your purchase offer.

QUESTIONS TO ASK SELLER-AGENT

Is There Any Lifting or Tearing in the Flooring?

☐ yes ☐ no

This may not be readily evident, particularly if it's in corner areas. Ask the seller to show you any problems. Ask why they occurred and why they have not been fixed. You may want to deduct the cost of repair from your offer.

How Recently Was the Flooring Replaced? Why?

☐ yes ☐ no

A good vinyl or linoleum floor will last 10 years or longer. If replaced, ask how old the previous flooring was. Was it damaged by water? If so, was the water problem fixed? Was the old flooring removed prior to laying the new (a good idea)? Was it done professionally?

What Is the Quality of the Flooring?

☐ yes ☐ no

It is not always possible to tell the quality of vinyl or linoleum flooring just by looking. Often, however, the seller can tell you the cost. Generally speaking, the higher the cost, the better. If the seller has extra pieces, ask for a small sample. You can then take this to a flooring store and quickly ascertain its true quality by comparing it to flooring available for sale.

Carpeting

QUESTIONS TO ASK YOURSELF

How Good Does It Look?

☐ yes   ☐ no

Carpeting that is high quality will look good. Unfortunately, carpeting that is poor quality, but that is brand new or has recently been cleaned, may look good, too. If the carpeting looks bad, it probably needs to be replaced. Figure anywhere from $10 a yard at the cheapest to $50 a yard and more at the top end to replace carpeting. It will cost between $3500 and $10,000 or more to replace the carpeting in a typical 2000-square-foot home.

How Thick Is the Pile?

☐ yes   ☐ no

Get down on your knees and separate the strands of fiber. Generally speaking, the thicker they are, the better the quality. Cheap carpeting will spread easily, revealing the backing beneath.

Is It Wall-to-Wall in Every Room?

☐ yes   ☐ no

Wall-to-wall carpeting needs to cover all the living areas (except kitchens where carpeting is a "no-no!" because of spills). Generally speaking, in homes with wall-to-wall carpeting there is only a subfloor beneath, meaning that if the carpeting doesn't cover, another type of flooring will have to fill the gap. If any subflooring shows, it may present an awkward and devaluing appearance.

Are There Different Colors in Different Rooms?

☐ yes ☐ no

Unless it's done as a fashion statement, the carpeting throughout should be the same color. Often bedrooms will have different colors and types of carpeting from the rest of the house because when the house was recarpeted, the owner tried to save money by not redoing the bedrooms. This is a devaluing factor.

Does It Feel Thick and Lush When You Step on It?

☐ yes ☐ no

The feel of the carpet comes from the padding. A solid thick padding will feel wonderful. A padding that is too thin or too soft will feel hard or mushy underfoot. Usually you cannot replace the padding without also replacing the carpeting.

Are There Any Stains or Discolorations?

☐ yes ☐ no

Sometimes these can be removed by cleaning. However, if the rest of the carpet looks clean, chances are the seller already tried this and was unsuccessful. This is particularly a problem in lighter-colored carpets. The only real alternative is to replace the carpeting in the entire room or in the entire home if you want all carpeting to match.

Any Burn Marks, Torn Corners, or Worn Areas?

☐ yes ☐ no

None of these can be fixed—the carpeting must be replaced. In particular, look for burns near fireplaces and sofas and worn areas in locations where people walk. High-traffic areas are the first to show wear.

QUESTIONS TO ASK SELLER-AGENT

How Old Is the Carpet?   ☐ yes   ☐ no

Average carpeting has a life span of between three to seven years, depending on quality and wear. If the seller says the carpeting is five years old, figure you'll have to replace it within the next couple of years.

What Type Is It?   ☐ yes   ☐ no

There are many different types of material used for carpeting. Generally speaking, nylon offers the most variety and the greatest resistance to wear at a lowest cost.

Does It Have Stain-Resistant Qualities?   ☐ yes   ☐ no

The federal government requires that most carpeting meet minimal stain-resistant standards. However, there's an enormous difference between minimal and best. In top grades of carpeting, the stain resistance is built right into the fibers. In lesser-quality carpeting, it is sprayed on during the production process. Ask the seller if he or she has a sample of the carpeting. There may be a label stating its stain resistance.

When Was It Last Cleaned?   ☐ yes   ☐ no

It's a common misconception that carpeting can be endlessly cleaned. More than half a dozen cleanings will usually significantly reduce its appearance. If the carpeting looks bad, ask when the seller-agent last cleaned it. If it was recently, it may be that the carpet has been over-cleaned and will no longer respond with a good appearance.

Are There Any Stains?

You may easily miss these yourself in a casual examination. Ask the owner about stains located under furniture and throw rugs. Ask if there has been an attempt to remove them and what was the result.

Any Cat or Dog Urine Stains?

This is perhaps the most important question. Cat and some dog urine stains often *cannot be removed!* Rather, the carpeting, the padding, and sometimes the flooring underneath must be replaced to get rid of the stain; otherwise odors will continually recur. A really cautious buyer will get down on all fours and go around the corners of each room sniffing the carpeting, regardless of what the seller-agent says! Consider not buying a home with pet urine stains, unless the seller agrees to recarpet.

Ceilings

QUESTIONS TO ASK YOURSELF

Are All Ceilings at Least Normal Height?

Eight feet is standard ceiling height. Anything less in a modern home suggests that the ceiling may have been constructed without the benefit of a building permit. In old homes, lower ceilings were common. Also, sloped ceilings that dip down to around seven feet in the corners are not uncommon in some modern construction. If a ceiling is suspiciously low, ask to see the construction permits.

If There Are Tall Ceilings, Is Heating Compensated? ☐ yes ☐ no

Tall ceilings are the rage. Unfortunately, they present difficult heating situations. Ducts close to floor level and ceiling fans help circulate heat and keep it from rising to where it is useless, near the ceiling.

Is There a "Popcorn" Spray on the Ceiling? ☐ yes ☐ no

In the 1960s and 1970s it was popular to spray ceilings with an "acoustical" mixture that looked like blown-on popcorn. Today it gives homes a dated look and tends to lower value. Removal can cost around $1 a square foot, if there's no asbestos in the mixture. When testing reveals that asbestos is present, the price goes up to between $5 and $10 a square foot, because of the hazardous nature of the removal (which should only be done by professionals).

Are Any Ceiling Cracks Evident? ☐ yes ☐ no

Some small cracks, particularly at corners, are normal as the house ages and settles. Cracks more than $\frac{1}{16}$ of an inch wide or running down or across the ceiling suggest serious structural problems. Have a structural engineer evaluate the property.

Is There Any Bowing of the Ceiling? ☐ yes ☐ no

This suggests too much weight on the roof (as from snow load). This can also occur in homes where a new and heavier roof has been added, and the structure isn't strong enough to support it. This is serious—get a structural inspection.

If There Are Beams, Are They in Good Shape?

☐ **yes** ☐ **no**

Exposed beams come and go as fashion statements. Check to see they aren't bowed, are well painted or stained, and don't show any obvious signs of pest infestation. Removal of faux beams is inexpensive, but usually requires replastering or retexturing and repainting the ceiling.

Are There Any Water Stains or Mold on the Ceiling?

☐ **yes** ☐ **no**

There should never be water stains on the ceiling. On the top floor they suggest roof leaks. On lower floors they suggest leaks from showers, tubs, or toilets on the upper floors.

QUESTIONS TO ASK SELLER-AGENT

Are There Any Problems with the Ceiling?

☐ **yes** ☐ **no**

You want a solid No answer. If you get anything else, be prepared to hire an inspector to check it out. Ceiling problems in themselves are usually minor, but they can suggest far more serious problems elsewhere.

Are There Any Leaks?

☐ **yes** ☐ **no**

What you want to know is whether there were some leaks that the seller has patched and that now don't show up. If so, ask who did the repair work (was it done professionally?). If the seller did it him- or herself, get the job inspected.

Walls and Wall Finishes

QUESTIONS TO ASK YOURSELF

Are There Any Holes in the Walls?

☐ yes   ☐ no

These are usually caused by lack of a door stopper where the door handle banged into the wall, or by someone putting a fist through. Patches can usually be quickly done by a handyperson for around $25 apiece. However, it may be difficult to match the texture and paint of the wall, so the damage may still be visible.

Are There Any Marks on the Walls?

☐ yes   ☐ no

Some marks, such as made by pencils, simple dirt, and other smudges can be removed by carefully spraying a solvent such as Fantastic,™ and rubbing lightly. Other marks, such as those made by crayons, grease, or many types of ink cannot be removed as easily. Usually the mark must be covered with a shellac spray to seal it and then the entire wall must be repainted. Figure around $100 a wall to have it professionally done.

Are There Any Cracks in the Walls?

☐ yes   ☐ no

Small cracks near corners are normal. Large cracks (more than $\frac{1}{16}$ inch wide) or running across walls (horizontally, diagonally, or vertically) suggest serious structural problems and should be professionally inspected.

Do Any Walls Need Painting?

☐ yes   ☐ no

Plan on painting in all but a brand-new home. Even if the walls look clean, after the seller moves his or her furniture out, there will be marks. Painting the interior of an entire house can start at around $2000. Normally the seller will *not* go for this.

Are the Walls Plumb?

☐ yes   ☐ no

Stand at a corner or edge and cast your eye along the wall. It should be straight and even. Walls that tilt in or out, bulge, or are concave indicate they were poorly constructed (or the home has seriously shifted). Have a professional inspector check it out.

Are the Walls Insulated?

☐ yes   ☐ no

Insulated walls are essential to efficiently heat or cool a home. Uninsulated walls are almost impossible to insulate, short of tearing out the wallboard and starting over. You may want to consider passing on an uninsulated house! If you can't easily see for yourself, ask a professional inspector. He or she will remove a wall socket plate and poke around behind it with a screwdriver, turning up insulation if there is any. *Don't do this yourself, as you risk serious electrical shock.*

QUESTIONS TO ASK SELLER-AGENT

Are There Any Holes or Marks in the Walls?   ☐ yes   ☐ no

You may have missed them. Have the seller point them out. If none, be sure you get it in writing.

Are There Any Cracks in the Walls?   ☐ yes   ☐ no

As noted above, cracks are more serious than marks or holes. Ask the seller if any inspectors have said that they indicate a structural problem. Ask how long they have been there. Did they occur after an earthquake? (If so, be sure to have the foundation thoroughly checked.)

Have There Been Any Wall Repairs? Where? By Whom?   ☐ yes   ☐ no

See what the repaired area looks like. If the seller did it and it looks bad, you may need to have a professional come in and do a better job. Be sure that it's part of your purchase offer.

Light Fixtures, Switches, and Plugs

QUESTIONS TO ASK YOURSELF

Is There a Light Fixture in Every Room?

☐ yes   ☐ no

You will want to have light in every room; hence, there should be a provision for a light fixture. There should either be a switch that controls a ceiling light, or a switch that controls a receptacle on a wall, into which a light can be plugged. Not having a light switch in a room is a sign of obsolescence and may indicate that the room was added without benefit of a building permit.

Is the Bathroom and Kitchen Lighting Adequate?

☐ yes   ☐ no

While low lights can suffice in other rooms, you want bright light in two areas: kitchen and baths. Typically the best lighting here comes from fluorescent lighting. Adding lighting to these areas is usually not expensive, under $500 for an electrician, plus the costs of the lights. The price can go up dramatically if there's no accessible attic space above.

Are There Any Energy-Saving Lights?

☐ yes   ☐ no

In these days of energy shortages, lighting that consumes less electricity is in great demand. Fluorescent lights usually consume only a fraction of the energy used by incandescents. Halogen lighting is the brightest, but tends to use the most energy. There are new high-tech tungsten lights that last many times longer than the other kinds, produce only a little less light than their cousins, yet consume a fraction of the energy. If you're not sure what kind of lights are in the home, ask the seller, who undoubtedly knows.

Will You Want to Replace the Light Fixtures?

☐ yes ☐ no

It's often the case that the buyer doesn't like the existing lighting. Be aware that light fixtures range in price from as little as $50 to well over $5000. Replacing is usually quite easy and if you can't do it, a handy-person usually can.

Do All the Light Switches Work?

☐ yes ☐ no

It's easy enough to check out. Simply turn them on in every room. A light should go on somewhere. If it doesn't, it could be because the switch controls a receptacle into which no lamp is plugged in. Ask the seller-agent about it.

Is There a Plug Every 12 Feet along the Walls?

☐ yes ☐ no

You don't have to measure. Just eyeball it. There should be a plug on every wall and the distance between them shouldn't be too great. The standard maximum distance between wall receptacles is 12 feet because the standard minimum cord length for lights and appliances is 6 feet—that way receptacles are conveniently located, and you don't have to use dangerous extension cords.

Are There GFI Plugs in Bathrooms and in the Kitchen?

☐ yes   ☐ no

GFI (Ground Fault Interruptor) plugs are a safety issue. They cut the power in an emergency, should you, for example, drop the hair dryer in the toilet. You can identify GFI plugs because they have little "test" and "reset" buttons. Just because a plug doesn't have this, however, does not necessarily mean it isn't linked to a GFI plug or circuit breaker elsewhere. The only way to know is to push the "test" on the GFI plug and then if the linked plugs go dead, chances are they are connected. To confirm this, push the "reset," and all plugs should be active again. It costs about $10 apiece for GFI plugs plus installation, which a handyperson or electrician can do.

Is There 220-V Service in the Kitchen and Utility Room?

☐ yes   ☐ no

This is important in case you want to use an electric stove, washer, or dryer. Even if you don't, it will be important to the next buyer and could affect the value of the property. Installing 220-V service can cost $1000 or more and requires the service of an electrician.

QUESTIONS TO ASK SELLER-AGENT

Any There Any Broken Lights, Switches, or Plugs?

☐ yes   ☐ no

Note them and then make sure that it's part of your purchase offer that they be replaced. It's usually not a big item and most sellers won't balk at this. But, as long as it needs doing, you might as well not have to do it yourself.

Are Any Switches or Receptacles Not in Service?

□ **yes**   □ **no**

Buyers are sometimes surprised to discover that some switches and receptacles do not work. Sometimes this is because they were never installed when the home was built. Other times it's because they were rerouted elsewhere as part of renovation work. And sometimes they are just decorative. There usually isn't a problem here, as long as you're not bothered by it and there's no electrical safety issue (check with your professional building inspector).

Are Any Fixtures Not Included in the Purchase?

□ **yes**   □ **no**

Sometimes sellers will specifically exclude chandeliers or other fixtures, even though they appear attached to walls or ceilings. If they can easily be detached, they can be removed and taken away. My suggestion is that you *always* specify in your purchase offer that all light fixtures are included in the price, no matter what the seller says. If the seller balks, then you can negotiate, and if the seller really wants to take that fixture, you might possibly even get a small price reduction out of it!

Kitchen Cabinets

QUESTIONS TO ASK YOURSELF

Are the Cabinets in Generally Good Shape?

☐ **yes**   ☐ **no**

The cabinets should look sharp. If stained, they should be even and fresh looking. If painted, they should look clean with no chips or faded areas. There should be no cracks, dents, or other defects. Replacing cabinets in a kitchen can easily cost $5000 to $10,000 for starters.

Are the Doors Solid or Hollow Core?

☐ **yes**   ☐ **no**

Tap lightly in the center of a cabinet door. You should hear and feel a solid thud that indicates a quality solid wood door. If there's a slight echo and the door vibrates, it indicates the doors are inexpensive hollow core.

Do They Look Modern?

☐ **yes**   ☐ **no**

Old-fashioned cabinets (typically in darker wood) can date a property. They can also drag down the value of the home.

Are They Up to the Standards of the Home?

☐ **yes**   ☐ **no**

If the kitchen has granite countertops and a fancy floor, you expect high-quality cabinets. If the cabinets are cheaper than what would be normal for the rest of the kitchen (or the house), they will drag the property's value down. You may find you'll want to replace them yourself later on. Take this into consideration when you make your purchase offer.

Are There Any Cabinet Doors That Don't Close Properly?

☐ yes ☐ no

Over time, cabinet doors will warp slightly and may not close completely. Usually a simple adjustment can remedy this. However, if the doors are heavily warped, it may be impossible to close them and they will need to be replaced. Replacing doors alone and refinishing existing cabinets costs about two-thirds the price of putting in new.

Is Any Hardware Broken or Missing?

☐ yes ☐ no

Sometimes a handle or two may be broken or missing. The problem is that if the house is older, it may be impossible to find exact replacements. This means that *all* the hardware will have to be replaced in order for it to match. Simple cabinet door handles can cost anywhere from a dollar to $20 and more apiece. Cabinet door hinges generally cost around a few dollars a set—much more for more fashionable pieces.

Are There Enough Kitchen Cabinets?

☐ yes ☐ no

This is a judgment call. You want enough cabinets to be able to handle all of your needs. Sometimes, particularly in inexpensive newer homes, there simply aren't enough. That means you'll have the cost of adding more.

QUESTIONS TO ASK SELLER-AGENT

Were the Cabinets Replaced? When?

☐ yes ☐ no

In homes more than 10 years old, this is a good question to ask. It may be that the cabinets look so fine because they are relatively new. This is a plus and adds value to the home.

Are There Any Problems with the Cabinets? ☐ yes ☐ no

There may be problems that aren't obvious at a casual glance. If the seller points out any broken doors, falling cabinets, or other problems, get an estimate from a cabinet maker on repair costs.

Kitchen Counters

QUESTIONS TO ASK YOURSELF

Is the Counter Type Appropriate for the Home? ☐ yes ☐ no

In order of cost, the most expensive countertops are granite; less expensive is Corian (or similar material), then tile, and the least expensive is laminate. A laminate countertop in a million-dollar home might affect the value adversely. A granite countertop in a $100,000 home might be overbuilding.

If Laminate, Are There Any Burns or Loose Areas? ☐ yes ☐ no

Burns cannot be repaired. Rather, the laminate in that area (often a large section) must be replaced. Sometimes as the laminate ages or if it wasn't installed properly, it will separate from its backing (usually pressed wood). Sometimes it can be reglued, sometimes not. A modest-sized laminate countertop can cost between $500 and $1000 installed.

If Tile Countertops, Any There Any Cracks or Broken Tiles?   ☐ yes   ☐ no

Tile will crack or chip if plates or other heavy objects are dropped on it. Cracks that extend across more than one tile suggest a problem with the base, which might only be corrected by replacing the countertop. The cost of replacing a few cracked or broken tiles is typically around $50, if you can find matching pieces. Ask the seller if he or she has any extra tiles. A whole new countertop can cost $1500 or much more, depending on the quality of the tile.

Is the Tile Old-Fashioned?   ☐ yes   ☐ no

Tile has been used in kitchens for centuries, and it never truly goes out of style. However, colors and patterns move in and out of fashion. An old style will date a home and adversely affect the property's value. A modern style will have just the opposite effect.

How Is the Grout?   ☐ yes   ☐ no

Often the grout will become stained over time. Cleaning with a mild vinegar or chlorine solution may help. Regrouting means removing the top layer of grout, putting fresh, clean grout on, and then sealing. The cost is typically around $400 or less for the entire countertop.

If Granite, Are There Any Stains or Cracks?   ☐ yes   ☐ no

If a granite countertop is not properly sealed, it can stain because granite is porous. Stains probably cannot be removed. Since cracks cannot be repaired, the entire piece of granite must be replaced. Granite countertops are sold by the inch—expect to pay $7000 and up for a typical kitchen.

If Corian, Are There Any Marks?

☐ yes ☐ no

This is a synthetic product that produces a seamless finish. It is hard to mar, but will burn. Burns can be cut out and a new material molded into place. The cost is typically a few hundred dollars for a repair. Expect to pay $5000 and up for a typical kitchen countertop.

QUESTIONS TO ASK SELLER-AGENT

How Old Is the Countertop?

☐ yes ☐ no

If it looks good, it may be a fairly recent renovation, which adds to the home's value. If it looks bad, it may be the original and can have the opposite effect.

Are There Any Problems with the Countertop?

☐ yes ☐ no

Replacement is sometimes necessitated by an improperly constructed base or because water got underneath. If this was the case, was the problem corrected before the countertop was replaced?

Kitchen Appliances

QUESTIONS TO ASK YOURSELF

Do All the Appliances Work?

☐ yes ☐ no

It is usually understood that the seller will deliver the home with all appliances working. This is a condition of having a home warranty policy issued (which protects you for a year after the sale against appliance failure). Be sure everything works, or will be working by the close of escrow.

Are The Appliances Modern or Old-Fashioned?

☐ yes ☐ no

Modern appliances make a kitchen sparkle. Old-fashioned appliances drag down the appearance and the value of the home. If you want to replace them yourself, figure around $2000 per kitchen for average quality, not including the refrigerator.

Are Any Appliances Scratched or Damaged?

☐ yes ☐ no

For tiny blemishes, touch-up paint may do the trick. For dents, large scratches, burns, or other defects, often the entire appliance must be replaced.

Is the Stove Gas or Electric?

☐ yes ☐ no

Some people prefer one, some the other. Check to see what electricity versus gas costs are in your area to be sure that you aren't buying into a high-cost appliance. Be sure you try it out to see that it's working.

Will You Be Happy with the Refrigerator?

☐ yes ☐ no

Only occasionally do refrigerators come with the home. If yours does, be sure you'll be happy with the size and amenities it offers. A new, large, side-by-side double-door refrigerator with water cooler and ice-maker starts at around $1000.

Is the Garbage Disposal at Least a Half Horsepower?

☐ yes ☐ no

The horsepower is written right on it. Anything less will not operate well and will constantly be clogging and stopping. A new disposal runs around $150 plus another $50 to $100 for installation. Turn it on to be sure it works.

Is There Instant Hot Water?

☐ yes ☐ no

This is usually a separate faucet (attached to a small heater and storage tank) that supplies instant hot water. It's a real plus and can add value to a home. Even better is a recirculating pump that delivers instant hot water to all hot faucets. Check to see that it works and that the water is hot (but don't burn yourself—it can come out close to boiling, depending on its setting!).

Is There a Trash Compactor?

☐ yes ☐ no

Again, this is not a necessity, but a value-added feature. Be sure the door closes properly and that it isn't scratched. Ask to see it in operation.

Is the Dishwasher Silent?

☐ yes   ☐ no

The cost of a dishwasher can be as little as a few hundred dollars and as much as several thousand. Often the difference is how quiet it is. (Most dishwashers do a fairly good job of washing.) An ultra-quiet dishwasher (it'll say so right on it!) is a value-added feature. Ask to see the owner's manual to determine just how quiet it is—sellers usually save these. Be sure you turn it on so you can see it in operation.

Is There a Built-in Microwave?

☐ yes   ☐ no

This is another value-added feature. While you can buy a stand-alone microwave for around $100, a built-in can easily cost $1000. Be sure you turn it on so you can see it in operation.

Any There Other Built-in Appliances?

☐ yes   ☐ no

Some homes offer built-in mixers, juicers, bread-makers, and a host of other appliances. These are extras that, while nice, do not add much value. Make sure they all function.

QUESTIONS TO ASK SELLER-AGENT

Do the Appliances Come with the House?

☐ yes   ☐ no

Surprisingly, almost all "built ins" simply unplug and can be removed. Be sure that all appliances are included in the sale. This should be written into the purchase agreement.

Are There Any Nonworking Appliances?

☐ yes   ☐ no

As noted, all appliances should work, and this should be a condition of the purchase. If something isn't working, ask the seller if it will be repaired or replaced. If replaced, be sure to insist that you have a voice in the choice (brand and model) of the replacement.

How Old Are the Appliances?

☐ yes   ☐ no

Appliances, in general, have a life span of about 10 to 15 years. If all the appliances are 15 years old, count on having to replace them all yourself within the next few years.

Bathroom Counters and Fixtures

QUESTIONS TO ASK YOURSELF

Are the Cabinets in Good Shape?

☐ yes   ☐ no

Does the paint and/or stain look good? Is the color appropriate to a bathroom (or will you want to repaint)? Ready-made bathroom cabinets cost around $250 apiece. Special orders cost twice as much or more.

Is the Countertop in Good Shape?

☐ **yes**   ☐ **no**

Often bathroom countertops are synthetic marble, which may get stains, cuts, and cracks over time. Replacement is inexpensive (several hundred dollars), but finding a top to match the cabinet can be difficult.

Is It Stylish?

☐ **yes**   ☐ **no**

Upgraded countertops of tile, Corian, or granite add value to the home and look good. The cost of installing new countertops varies from around $500 to $10,000, or more.

Do All the Cabinet Doors and Drawers Close?

☐ **yes**   ☐ **no**

Try them. If they don't work, look at them edge-on to see if they are warped. Badly warped doors must be replaced. However, in bathrooms that usually means replacing both the cabinet, the countertop, sink, and faucets. Figure at least $1000 or much more, depending on the quality you choose.

Is There Any Mold or Mildew?

☐ **yes**   ☐ **no**

Look inside the cabinet for this. Sometimes you have to move some things around to see into the back of the cabinet. Occasionally a mold or mildew problem cannot be cured by painting, but requires the replacement of the cabinet.

Is There a Medicine Cabinet?

☐ yes ☐ no

A medicine cabinet is a requirement of every bathroom, yet some do not have one. A common medicine cabinet only costs around $30, but finding a place to put it can be difficult. Installation can cost around $100.

Is There Adequate Lighting? Is It Stylish?

☐ yes ☐ no

Many municipalities require fluorescent lighting in bathrooms for adequate light. If tungsten, there should be enough bulbs (or large enough ones) to brightly light the room. Activities like shaving require adequate lighting. New fixtures can be purchased for well under $100. Installation, however, particularly if new wiring must be run and new switches installed, can cost far more.

Is There a Large Mirror?

☐ yes ☐ no

In addition to the medicine cabinet, a well-outfitted bathroom will also include a large mirror. Is it of good quality (no distortions, not damaged, bright)? A good bathroom mirror can easily cost $100.

Is There Enough Storage Space?

☐ yes ☐ no

Lack of storage space is always a problem in bathrooms. The more storage space, the better. If not inside the bathroom, look for a nearby linen closet where towels and other bathroom supplies can be kept.

QUESTIONS TO ASK SELLER-AGENT

Are There Any Problems with Bathroom Counters or Fixtures?

☐ yes   ☐ no

Ask if any have recently been replaced. If so, why? Ask to see the receipts so you can determine the quality of the new items.

Are There Any Water Leaks in the Cabinet?

☐ yes   ☐ no

This can be a real problem if a faucet leaks and the water drains and sits in the cabinet. Mold and mildew can grow, which can be difficult to remove, sometimes requiring replacement of the cabinet.

Bathroom Plumbing Fixtures

QUESTIONS TO ASK YOURSELF

Do All the Faucets Work?

☐ yes   ☐ no

They should turn on; then they should turn off, *completely*. The hot water should come on fairly quickly. Try them all yourself. If something doesn't work, insist on a professional inspection. Replacing faucets can easily run from $100 to $1000, depending on quality.

Is There Enough Water Pressure?

☐ yes   ☐ no

Turn on all the bathroom faucets simultaneously. The water should continue to flow slowly. If it drops to a trickle, it suggests problems with the plumbing. (See Chapter 4, "Infrastructure.")

Do All the Drains Work?

☐ yes   ☐ no

Run the water in the tub, shower, and sink(s) for a time. It should continue to drain rapidly. Any backing up suggests a plugged line. It could be as simple as rooting it out (under $200), or having to replace a plugged line ($500 to $1500 and up).

Do the Drain Stoppers in the Tub and Sink Work?

☐ yes   ☐ no

The stopper should immediately prevent water from draining. When released, the water should flow out quickly. A plumber can usually correct simple problems for around $50 apiece.

Does the Toilet Work?

☐ yes   ☐ no

Flush the toilet at least three times. Look to see that the water flows out as quickly the last time as the first. Check around the base of the toilet for leaks. Make sure that after each cycle, the toilet completely stops water from coming in. Replacing the plumbing in a toilet can run around $50 for a simple job. Replacing the toilet can run from $100 to $1000, depending on quality (provided you can find a new toilet with a footprint similar to the old one). It can cost much more to fix plugged drains.

Is There Any Scaling, Peeling, or Deterioration on Any Faucets? ☐ yes ☐ no

Sometimes this can be cleaned with a mild vinegar solution. Usually, however, the faucets must be replaced. A low-cost faucet fixture runs around $50. High-quality fixtures start at around $500 and go up from there . . . plus installation.

Is the Fixture Quality Low, Standard, or High? ☐ yes ☐ no

Knowing this comes from experience. However, low-cost fixtures generally look cheap and are small. High-quality fixtures often are made of gold, silver, or other rare metals. The better the quality of the fixtures, the more valuable the home.

Are All Towel Racks and/or Hangers in Good Shape? ☐ yes ☐ no

Sometimes these are put into wallboard with molly bolts, which may loosen, making big holes in the plaster. It's mostly a nuisance. A handyperson can usually fix it for around $25, plus the cost of the fixture.

Are There Any Cracks, Breaks, or Chips in the Sinks or Tubs? ☐ yes ☐ no

A cheap sink costs under $25; a quality sink can cost as much as $250. A cheap plastic tub is around $125; a quality metal tub can cost $500 and up (particularly if it includes a whirlpool). Replacement is usually quite expensive, because of the need to rip out the old tub and then repair the enclosure. Often is possible to refinish the sink or tub in place for a fraction of the cost. Check with a good plumber.

Is There a Glass Enclosure for Tub or Shower?

☐ yes ☐ no

Quality construction will always have glass enclosures; low-cost construction will use curtains. Installing a tub-shower glass door will run around $500, including labor, more for a higher-quality unit. Be sure to check the corners to see if it has a safety glass label.

Are the Soap Dishes Attached to Walls?

☐ yes ☐ no

These are sometimes pulled loose. When they are, it can be difficult to reaffix them. Figure at least $50 and possibly as high as $100 or more to have soap dishes fixed.

Are There Any Water Stains Indicating Leaks?

☐ yes ☐ no

These water stains need to be thoroughly investigated by a professional. It might be nothing more than the replacement of a 35-cent washer. Or the problem could be deteriorated pipe costing thousands to replace.

QUESTIONS TO ASK SELLER-AGENT

Are There Any Leaks in the Bathroom?

☐ yes ☐ no

The seller should be able to tell you. If there are, ask if they were repaired and by whom. Also, ask what was the cause of the leak. If anything more than a washer, insist that it be professionally inspected.

Are There Any Faucets or Fixtures That Are Not Working? ☐ **yes** ☐ **no**

Sometimes there are "trick" faucets or toilets or other fixtures that work intermittently. If the seller identifies a problem, have it checked out.

Are There Any Problems with Drains (Toilet, Shower, or Sink)? ☐ **yes** ☐ **no**

There might be an obstruction in a drain that doesn't reveal itself when you run the water a short time. Ask if the location of the problem has been identified and what steps the seller has taken to correct the problem. Make the complete repair of the drain(s) a condition of your purchase.

Bathroom Tile, Ceilings, Walls, and Floors

QUESTIONS TO ASK YOURSELF

Are There Any Cracks in the Tile? Are Any Tiles Missing? ☐ **yes** ☐ **no**

Missing or cracked tile must be replaced. However, it may be difficult to find matching tiles, unless the seller has some extras. Broken or cracked tiles in a shower may indicate a water problem with the shower pan. Ask a professional inspector to check it out.

Is There Any Peeling Paint?

☐ yes   ☐ no

Moist heat from the tub or shower often causes paint to peel. This requires scraping and repainting. Because of the usually tight quarters, figure a couple of hundred dollars to have a professional paint the bathroom.

Is There Any Mildew or Black Mold?

☐ yes   ☐ no

Moisture can cause black mold or mildew to grow in the bathroom. Sometimes it can be removed with commercially available mold or mildew sprays. However, often it requires scraping, cleaning, and then repainting with an oil-based paint that has a strong antifungal ingredient. Figure a couple of hundred dollars for this at minimum.

Are There Any Holes in Walls or Ceilings?

☐ yes   ☐ no

These must be patched. Small holes can easily be fixed by a handyperson for under $50. Large holes may require adding new wallboard, taping, and texturing. Figure $250 and up for a professional-looking job.

Is There Any Discoloration in the Flooring?

☐ yes   ☐ no

You're looking for water damage. Though it might be dry when you're there, past water leaking could have caused fungal growth under the flooring. Be sure to alert the termite and professional home inspector to check for this, if you see anything suspicious.

Is Any Tile or Linoleum Loose?

☐ yes   ☐ no

Loose tiles or linoleum that curls up at the edges also suggests water underneath. Tap on tiles to see if they adhere solidly to floor, or do they sound hollow because they are just lying there loose. A new bathroom floor can cost between $300 and $1000 or more, depending on materials and installation.

QUESTIONS TO ASK SELLER-AGENT

Have You Had Any Problems in the Past with Mold or Mildew?

☐ yes   ☐ no

The seller may have simply painted over it. If a problem is reported, ask how it was corrected. If the fungus was not properly removed prior to painting and if an antifungal paint was not used, it will almost certainly come back. Deduct the cost of a good fix from your purchase offer.

Are There Any Leaks?

☐ yes   ☐ no

They might not be evident now, but could have been serious before. Ask the seller if a professional corrected them and, if so, can you see the invoice. If the seller corrected them, be sure to have the home inspector check the repair out thoroughly.

Mirrors

QUESTIONS TO ASK YOURSELF

Are Mirrors Permanently Affixed?

☐ **yes**   ☐ **no**

Mirrors that are glued to walls or ceilings normally will come with the home. Mirrors, regardless of size, that are simply hung on walls normally will not. To be sure that you get any mirrors that you want, specifically include them as part of the purchase offer.

Are There Door Mirrors?

☐ **yes**   ☐ **no**

Check to make sure that mirrors on sliding doors or on bedroom closet doors are safety glass. Otherwise, slamming the door could break the mirror causing dangerous shards to fly out. Replacement of a door mirror with new safety glass can easily cost $250 and up.

Are There Ceiling Mirrors?

☐ **yes**   ☐ **no**

If mirrors are hung on the ceiling, be sure they are permanently and solidly affixed. Mirrors are glass, and they weigh far more than other ceiling coverings—if they fall, they can seriously injure a person. Look for edges that are hanging loose; if necessary, get on a chair to carefully see if a ceiling mirror is loose.

Are the Mirrors Made in One Piece or in Panels?

☐ yes ☐ no

Floor-to-ceiling mirrors may either be a single piece or made up of panels. Paneled mirrors are less expensive to replace—solid mirrors look better.

Any Any Mirrors Scratched, Peeling, or Broken?

☐ yes ☐ no

A mirror that is scratched or broken should be replaced. The reflection that a mirror gives comes from its back coating. If this peels, as happens with older mirrors, it will look bad. Be sure to have damaged mirrors replaced by the seller.

QUESTIONS TO ASK SELLER-AGENT

Are Any Mirrors Broken or Damaged?

☐ yes ☐ no

You may not have time to carefully examine all mirrors. Have the seller give you an overall statement that none are damaged. If some are, have the seller replace them. If none are, be sure the seller puts it in writing.

Fireplaces and Heaters

QUESTIONS TO ASK YOURSELF

Does the Fireplace Have a Screen?

☐ yes ☐ no

These can be difficult to install and can easily cost several hundred dollars. If there's one already there, be sure that it's included in the purchase price of the home. Open and close it to be sure it works. If it's broken, ask that it be fixed by the seller, or replaced.

Does It Have a Glass Door?

☐ yes ☐ no

A glass door on a fireplace helps radiate heat into the room, instead of letting it escape up the chimney, as a screen does. Check for cracks and discolorations in the glass. If there are any, ask that the glass door be fixed or replaced.

Does the Flue Move Easily?

☐ yes ☐ no

Usually found just inside the fireplace at the top, the flue opens and closes the chimney. Without getting too dirty, you can determine if it is functional by trying to move it back and forth. To see if it works, you will get dirty because you have to lie down with your head in the fireplace, shine a flashlight up, and move the handle—you'll see the flue open and close.

Are There Any Fireplace Tools?

☐ yes   ☐ no

These are usually personal property and go with the seller. However, they can cost anywhere from $50 to $250. You can try to get the seller's by demanding that they be included in the purchase price.

Does the Fireplace Burn Gas?

☐ yes   ☐ no

A gas outlet will allow you the option of burning gas logs, or even of just using the gas to help start a wood fire. There should be a valve in a handy location to operate the gas and a burner underneath the grate. Remember, however, that gas prices these days are sometimes higher than wood!

Is There a Gas Insert in the Fireplace?

☐ yes   ☐ no

Today this usually consists of a high-tech gas heater installed into the fireplace opening. It burns a small amount of gas quite efficiently and radiates heat into the home. It can produce as much as 10 times more heat than a regular fireplace! Usually a gas insert will cost around $1500 to $2000 plus installation.

Are There Any Cracks Visible Anywhere in the Fireplace?

☐ yes   ☐ no

Cracks can be a serious health hazard, as they can allow toxic fumes to escape from the fireplace into the living quarters of the house. A qualified fireplace professional should be hired to examine any cracks. Replacing a masonry fireplace can easily cost $7500 or more.

Are There Any Gas Heaters in the Rooms?

☐ yes   ☐ no

These are usually baseboard or wall units. Because they are peripherally located, their ability to heat large areas is restricted. Typically they are very inefficient, must run a long time to heat the home, and, as a result, are very costly to operate. Be sure that there is a convenient switch to turn them on and off. Turn them on to see if they work. Replacing these with central heating can cost $2500 and up.

Are There Electric Heaters?

☐ yes   ☐ no

Electricity is the least efficient way to heat a home. Electric heaters are sometimes found in baseboard, ceiling, or floor units. Most families find they cannot afford to run electric heaters regularly during the winter. Plan on replacing them as soon as possible.

What About Radiators?

☐ yes   ☐ no

Fifty years ago it was not uncommon to have a boiler in the basement that ran on gas, coal, or oil, supplying steam to radiators throughout the entire house. Today, a water circulation system can do the same thing. It's usually found along the baseboard of a room, with the heating plant in a central location. It may be oil- or gas-fired and, depending on the cost of oil or gas, can be an inexpensive and highly efficient heating system.

Is There a Thermostat to Control Heaters?

☐ yes   ☐ no

Whatever type of heating is in the house, it should be thermostatically controlled. Manually turning the heater on and off will result in broad temperature spreads. A new digital thermostat only costs around $50, so as long as there's some thermostat wiring in place; you can usually upgrade cheaply.

Why Are There Heaters if There Is Also Central Heating?

☐ yes   ☐ no

Except in rural areas where two separate forms of heating may be required, duplication of heating usually means that one or both systems are inadequate. You may want to consider installing a brand-new, high-efficiency system.

Is There a Carbon Monoxide Detector Installed?

☐ yes   ☐ no

Whenever there is combustion, as occurs in gas-, oil-, or coal-fired heaters, carbon monoxide is produced. Normally, it is safely vented outdoors. However, a faulty heat exchanger can send it into the house. A detector is the only way to know if this problem exists. If one is not present, plan on buying it—the cost is around $50.

QUESTIONS TO ASK SELLER-AGENT

When Was the Chimney Last Cleaned?

☐ yes   ☐ no

If the fireplace is used at all, the chimney needs to be cleaned. The cleaning only needs to be done once a year, but if not cleaned, a chimney fire can occur, which can potentially burn down the house. Ask to see the receipt for the last chimney cleaning.

If Any New Work Was Done, Was There a Building Permit?

☐ yes   ☐ no

If a seller adds a door or an alcove without a building permit, it's unlikely there will be health and safety problems. But working on a fireplace or heater, especially one involving gas, is another matter. All such work should be done only by permit and with building department inspection. If not, demand that it be brought up to code and inspected. If the seller refuses, demand that the system be removed and replaced with a permitted one, or refuse to buy the home.

Are There Any Cracks, Defects, or Other Known Problems?

☐ yes   ☐ no

Problems may exist that you cannot see. However, the seller may know about them. If you are told of any, assume the worst and demand a professional inspection to determine how serious the problems are and what remedies are available.

How Big an Area Does the Fireplace and/or Heater Heat?

☐ yes   ☐ no

Remember that fireplaces typically exhaust 90 percent of their heat up the chimney. Likewise, wall heaters are only locally effective. The seller will often know how wide a swath of area is heated. Determine if this is enough to keep you warm on the coldest days, or if you'll need an additional heating system.

Crawl Space

QUESTIONS TO ASK YOURSELF

What Is a Crawl Space?

☐ yes ☐ no

A crawl space is an open area between the first floor of a home and the ground. Because it is shallow, often no more than 18 to 30 inches high, it is called a "crawl" space—the only way you can gain entrance is to crawl in. It typically covers the entire bottom of the home.

Should I Crawl into It?

☐ yes ☐ no

That's up to you. You may find anything from spiders to toads to mushrooms. If you do go, plan on wearing old clothing. And be prepared to crawl around on your belly and back. Oh, and bring a good flashlight. Probably the best time to get a good look in the crawl space is to accompany a professional home inspector (later on, after your offer has been accepted) who can lead the way and point out any dangers as well as problems.

What Can I See from the Opening?

☐ yes ☐ no

You may be able to see much more from the opening than you think. Be sure to take a strong flashlight to shine in. And let your eyes get used to the darkness; otherwise, on a bright day you won't be able to see anything.

Is There Adequate Ventilation?

☐ yes ☐ no

There should be a screened vent every 6 to 8 feet. This allows air to circulate in the crawl space and prevents moisture buildup. Check to see that there are vents from the outside. Then, check to see that they aren't blocked from the inside. They should be quite evident from the light shining through them.

Is There Any Standing Water?

☐ yes ☐ no

You won't be able to see the entire area from the opening, but you may be able to see a long way. There should be no standing water anywhere. If there is, insist on a soils inspection and have a contractor tell you how the problem can be alleviated. Have the seller pay for the correction.

Are There Any Watermarks?

☐ yes ☐ no

Shine your light on the piers and the foundation. Are there any watermarks? If there are, they indicate that there was standing water in the past, and suggest possible water problems in the future.

Is There Any Insulation Hanging Loose?

☐ yes ☐ no

Most newer homes have the floors insulated, particularly in cold climates. The insulation should be up tight against the floor. Any hanging down will need to be rehung or replaced. It's not expensive, probably no more than a few hundred bucks.

Are There Any Broken or Hanging Loose Vents?

☐ yes   ☐ no

In many homes, vents under the floor carry heat. These should be supported by straps and not laying on the ground where they can absorb cold and are more likely to get damaged. If any are down, have a heating installer come out to give you a bid on getting them put back into place. Have the seller pay for correction.

Are There Any Sagging Plumbing Lines?

☐ yes   ☐ no

Both potable and waste water lines are under the home. If you see any, they should be strapped tight up against the flooring. If any are sagging or fallen on the ground, it could affect sewer drainage. Have them checked by a plumber. Have the seller correct the problem.

Is Any Electrical Wiring Hanging Down?

☐ yes   ☐ no

This can be a real hazard, particularly if there is standing water. If you see electrical writing hanging down in the crawl space, don't investigate it yourself—it could be dangerous. Have an electrician evaluate it. And then have the seller correct it.

QUESTIONS TO ASK SELLER-AGENT

Have You Ever Gone into the Crawl Space?

☐ yes   ☐ no

Some have, some haven't. If a seller has, ask why. Usually people don't go there just for the fun of it. Find out if there was a problem that led the seller to go under the home.

What Did You Find? How Was It Corrected?

This is a key question. If there was a problem underneath, find out what it was and what the seller did to alleviate it. Ask for reports and invoices. You want to be sure the job was done right the first time and won't recur.

Are There Any Problems under the House?

This is a catch-all question. Most sellers will indicate either "No" or "Don't know." If a seller indicates there is a problem, have it thoroughly evaluated, even if the seller indicates, "It's nothing!"

The Basement

QUESTIONS TO ASK YOURSELF

Should the Home Have a Basement?

On the East Coast the answer is certainly yes. On the West Coast, it's just as certainly no! You want a basement where it's common to have one, not where it isn't. Not having a basement on the East Coast can reduce the value of the home. Having one on the West Coast adds little to nothing to the value. Note: In New England, a *basement* is called a *cellar*.

Are the Washer and/or Dryer in the Basement? ☐ yes ☐ no

This is commonly the case in an older home. It means you'll have to trudge the laundry up and down the steps every time you want to wash and again to transfer the clothes to the dryer. It is far better to have the washer and/or dryer on the same level as the bedrooms or near the kitchen.

Is the Furnace or Water Heater in the Basement? ☐ yes ☐ no

Again, this is common in older homes. (In newer homes the space heater and water heater are frequently on the first floor—sometimes the space heater may be in the attic.) This takes up basement space that could otherwise be used as living area. If it's an oil-fired furnace, fumes may prevent other usage of the basement.

Is the Entire Basement below Ground Level? Is It Large? ☐ yes ☐ no

To save costs and sometimes because of soil or grading constraints, only a half-basement will be built. The bottom half below ground will be concrete; the top half above ground will be conventional wood walls. This requires two separate kinds of water and heat-cold insulation. Have a professional inspector check that it was done correctly.

Is the Basement Finished? Was It Done Well? ☐ yes ☐ no

Homes often come with an unfinished basement. The owner then finishes it off. Sometimes, however, it's a cheap and badly done job. If the basement was not finished well, figure you'll have to rip out what's there and redo everything to get it right. A basement of 1000 square feet can easily cost $10,000 or more to correctly finish off.

Can It Be Finished? Is the Floor Cement?

☐ yes ☐ no

Be sure you can finish off an unfinished basement. Dirt floors, standing water, or local building codes can make this impractical. Check with a contractor and with the local building department.

Is There Any Moisture in the Basement?

☐ yes ☐ no

Basements should be dry and dusty. If they have moisture, it probably indicates that the walls and floor were not built properly. An impermeable membrane should be behind walls and under the floor to keep moisture out. And drains should have been installed to keep rain runoff from entering the basement. Retrofitting is very expensive and can involve putting in a new basement floor and walls.

Is There Any Standing Water in the Basement?

☐ yes ☐ no

This could come from runoff and lack of drains, as indicated above. Or it could suggest a high water table. If a high water table is the problem, the only solution may be a permanent sump pump . . . or the basement cannot be used. Get opinions and estimates from a soils engineer and a contractor.

Are There Any Watermarks on the Basement Walls?

☐ yes ☐ no

Even though the basement may currently be dry, watermarks suggest that there was standing water at other times of the year. Question the seller. Ask the agent about a high water table, flooding, or other problems common in the area.

Are Any Cracks Evident in the Basement Floor or on the Walls? ☐ yes ☐ no

All concrete should have been poured with rebars (reinforcement steel bars) or heavy wire mesh inside to help keep the concrete from cracking. Tiny cracks (less than 1/16 inch) are common. A professional home inspector should investigate cracks that are any bigger.

Is There Adequate Heating and Lighting? ☐ yes ☐ no

Getting power and heat to a basement can be difficult. Sometimes sellers who renovate simply leave this out. If you have to retrofit it, figure on spending several thousand dollars.

Is There Adequate Ventilation? ☐ yes ☐ no

There should be plenty of windows, if part of the basement is above ground, to provide cross-ventilation and to dry out moisture. If the basement is entirely below ground, a forced air system will usually handle the task of circulation and ventilation. Be wary of a basement that's entirely below ground level with no ventilation of any kind. Even in a dry climate, it will be subject to moisture build-up and fungus growth.

QUESTIONS TO ASK SELLER-AGENT

Who Finished the Basement?

☐ yes   ☐ no

If it was a professional, get the original estimate and the invoice. Call the builder if you have any questions. If it was the homeowner, ask if it was done with a permit. The original plans will be on file at the building department. If it was done without a permit, consider asking the seller to bring it up to code. This, however, could be a deal breaker if the cost is excessive, as well it might be.

Are There Any Water (or other) Problems in the Basement?

☐ yes   ☐ no

Sometimes sellers will paint over watermarks on walls and cover up moisture with heavy carpeting. Get it in writing if the seller says no to this question. If the seller volunteers that there is a problem, have it thoroughly investigated.

Stairways

QUESTIONS TO ASK YOURSELF

How Wide Are the Stairs?

☐ yes   ☐ no

Stairs should be around 3 feet wide at minimum. This allows enough room for even a heavyset person to use them and also makes it easier to carry furniture up and down. Narrow stairs are a safety hazard and may not be up to current building code. Have a professional inspector check them if you're not sure.

How Steep Are They?

☐ yes   ☐ no

Necessity and local building codes determine the steepness of stairs. However, for practical purposes, simply see if they seem too steep for you. If so, you may want to look for a different house. You really can't change stairs (not very easily, anyhow) and you'll be going up and down them every day.

Is There Adequate Headroom?

☐ yes   ☐ no

There should be at least 8 feet of headroom above every stair. Less than that may be a safety hazard (tall people will always be banging their heads), and the stairs may not meet building code standards. If you're not sure, have a professional inspector check it out.

Are There Adequate Railings?

☐ yes   ☐ no

There should be a railing on at least one side of every stairway, especially on any side that's open to another area. The railing should be approximately 3 feet high and it should have slats, bars, balusters, or other devices placed no less than 4 inches apart to prevent children from falling or climbing through. You can easily measure this yourself. If it's off, have it checked and, if necessary, have the seller bring it up to local building code standards.

Are the Stairs in a Logical Place?

☐ yes   ☐ no

Sometimes the stairs are right behind the front door. Or they could be in a hallway. Or lead out of a bedroom. Poor architectural design is often seen most clearly in the location of stairways. Short of remodeling the whole house (read very expensive), you should probably pass on this house and buy one that has a better design.

If Carpeted, Is the Carpeting Adequately Tacked Down?   ☐ yes   ☐ no

Loose carpeting can cause falls. Usually you'll need a professional to do it right. For a simple tack job, the cost shouldn't be much more than $50 to $100.

Are There Any Loose Stairs?   ☐ yes   ☐ no

This is more serious and indicates that the stairs may not have been properly installed. Have a contractor check it out.

QUESTIONS TO ASK SELLER-AGENT

Are There Any Squeaky or Loose Stairs or Loose Carpeting?   ☐ yes   ☐ no

The seller should know. If the answer is no, get it in writing. If yes, have a carpet layer or contractor check it out.

Are There Any Problems with the Stairs?   ☐ yes   ☐ no

This is another catch-all question. You want a negative answer. Anytime the seller-agent says there is a problem, be sure you have it professionally checked out.

The Attic

QUESTIONS TO ASK YOURSELF

Does the Home Have an Attic?

☐ yes   ☐ no

Many homes do not. An attic is an asset as it provides an air buffer to help insulate the home. It also provides a crawl space that gives you access to the underside of the roof and the top side of the ceiling, which can be very helpful in the event of problems.

Is There Access? Can You See In?

☐ yes   ☐ no

Typically, access will be through a door cut into a closet ceiling. Or, it may be hidden behind a hallway light. (If the light is a large, rectangular panel, chances are there is access behind it.) Usually you'll need a ladder to see in. By just standing on the ladder, you can often see most of the attic without actually climbing inside. (If you do climb inside, stand *only* on the rafters. Standing on the ceiling itself will cause you to fall through resulting in serious injury or worse, not to mention ruining the ceiling!)

Do You See Spots of Light on the Underside of the Roof?

☐ yes   ☐ no

When you look up you want to see darkness. Spots of light indicate holes in the roof. Any small openings suggest a roof that is completely shot. Have a roofer check it out.

Do You See Any Watermarks?

☐ **yes** ☐ **no**

Watermarks on wood indicate a leaking roof. However, it may have been fixed in the past, yet the watermarks remain. Sometimes the only way to tell is to wait for the next big rainstorm. Ask the seller.

Do You See Any Burn Marks or Charred Wood?

☐ **yes** ☐ **no**

Attic fires are more common than most people realize. Often charred wood that is not severely weakened will remain. Have a professional inspector check it out to be sure that there are no weak beams. Ask the seller about damage and how it was repaired.

Do You See Lots of Insulation?

☐ **yes** ☐ **no**

You should. The thicker and denser the insulation, the better. In mild climates a minimum of 4 to 5 inches may be all that's needed. In severe hot or cold climates, insulation 10 to 15 inches thick may be needed. Ask a professional inspector what's right for your area and if the roof is fully insulated. (Sometimes the insulation will be piled high by the access door, yet very little is placed near the edges of the attic.) This may require that new insulation be blown in. The cost is usually under $500.

Do You See a Furnace and Ducts?

☐ **yes** ☐ **no**

Furnaces are often in the attic along with the ductwork. This is more efficient, but also is likely to produce more vibration and noise when the furnace is turned on.

Do You See Vents?

☐ yes   ☐ no

All attics must be ventilated to prevent moisture buildup and wood rot. You should see light coming in from many vents along the bottom edges of the roof as well as from several roof vents. Lack of proper venting can destroy your attic and roof. Installing vents is usually inexpensive, under $1000.

Does Anything Appear Unusual?

☐ yes   ☐ no

Does the seller store lots of things in the attic? This can be inviting to rodents as well as a fire hazard. Are there TV antennas in the attic? Sometimes owners will install them there when local code prohibits them from being on roofs. Not a problem, except that it impedes movement through the attic. Anything unusual should be brought to the attention of a professional home inspector. Also, ask the seller.

QUESTIONS TO ASK SELLER-AGENT

Are There Any Leaks in the Attic?

☐ yes   ☐ no

The seller should know. If the answer is no, get it in writing. If yes, ask how they were repaired and by whom. Ask to see estimates, invoices, and building permits. (It's often not necessary to secure a building permit just to fix an attic leak.)

Was the Attic Ever Strengthened to Accommodate a New Roof?   ☐ yes   ☐ no

Sometimes owners will replace an old wood, asphalt, or fiberglass roof with a heavier tile or cement shingle roof. To do this, however, the structure of the attic must usually be strengthened. Sometimes, however, this is only minimally done and eventually the attic fails, causing the roof to bow or in a worst case, crash! Have it professionally inspected by a roofer to be sure.

Were There Any Fires in the Attic?   ☐ yes   ☐ no

Ask the extent of the damage. What caused the fire? Who did the repairs (get estimates and invoices)? Was any suggested work not done? Why? Is there any work remaining to be done?

Is There Any Loose Wiring in the Attic?   ☐ yes   ☐ no

Owners will sometimes string wires to provide lighting in the attic or to install lights, switches, or plugs in the house. Ask if any work was done professionally. Did the seller get a permit (always required)? If not, insist that the owner get a permit and bring the work up to code.

Are There Any Other Problems in the Attic?   ☐ yes   ☐ no

This is a catch-all question in case there's something wrong that you didn't think to ask about. If the seller says no, get it in writing. If the seller says yes, have the problem(s) professionally investigated.

2
Exterior

Exterior Maintenance and Color

QUESTIONS TO ASK YOURSELF

Is the Paint Bright or Dull?
☐ yes   ☐ no

A well-maintained paint job will be bright and sharp looking. Paint that is dull, covered with paint dust, or otherwise looks flat probably needs to be redone. Plan on spending $3000 and up to have the exterior of a home completely repainted.

Are There Stains on the Paint?
☐ yes   ☐ no

Wood, nails, or other metals can stain paint; even some plants can stain paint. Spot repainting is usually not possible because of the difficulty of matching existing aged paint to new. Usually, at a minimum, an entire wall will need to be repainted. The cost will run from $100 to $500.

Is There Any Scaling or Peeling on the Paint?

☐ yes   ☐ no

This indicates bad application, particularly if there is scaling or peeling on wood trim. Usually the old paint must be scraped off before new can be applied. Scraping and sanding can add $1000 or more to the cost of a new paint job. (Burning off old paint is now considered a health risk and should not be done.)

If the House Is Stucco, Are There Any Cracks or Damage?

☐ yes   ☐ no

Stucco is not much more than Portland cement. If hit or jiggled (as in an earthquake), it can crack or pieces can break off. Patching is usually possible, if the area is small. Figure $250 for a tiny patch, $1000 and up if the whole house needs patching.

Are There Any Masonry Cracks?

☐ yes   ☐ no

The home may have brick, stone, cement, or other masonry facia. Small cracks can sometimes be patched. Cracks larger than ¹⁄₁₆ inch may indicate structural damage and should be thoroughly investigated by a structural engineer.

Are There Any Masonry Separations?

☐ yes   ☐ no

Stucco, cement, bricks, stone, and other masonry can separate from its backing. Again, this should be investigated for structural damage. While a filling can sometimes be used to fix small separations, a large separation (more than ½ inch) may require complete replacement of the masonry. Get a mason's estimate, but expect it to be in the thousands of dollars.

If the House Is Wood, Is There Any Cracking or Curling?   ☐ yes   ☐ no

Properly primed, then painted or stained wood will look good for a long time. If wood is cracked or curled, it indicates water has penetrated the covering coat. If not severe, it can be sanded and repainted or restained. If severe, it must be replaced. Costs vary enormously with the amount of wood replacement required. Recent increases in the cost of wood make it among the most expensive exterior home covering. To replace the exterior siding of a large house with wood can cost $10,000 or more.

If the Wood Is Stained, Are There Any Dried-Out Areas?   ☐ yes   ☐ no

Wood needs to be stained and then restained every other year or so. Dried-out areas (where there appears to be no stain) indicate the maintenance schedule was not followed. Applying new stain (figure slightly more than for repainting) will prevent new damage, but not cure existing damage.

Are There Any Unpainted and/or Unstained Areas?   ☐ yes   ☐ no

With the exception of masonry such as rocks or bricks, all exterior areas of the home should be painted or stained. If any are not, count on having to do that work yourself.

Are There Any Leaking Hose Bibs?   ☐ yes   ☐ no

There should be a hose bib at minimum at the front and rear of the home. Depending on location, if they are dripping and can't be fully turned off, they may result in stains and water damage to the exterior (not to mention a higher water bill). Figure $50 apiece to have them replaced.

QUESTIONS TO ASK SELLER-AGENT

When Was the Home Last Painted and/or Stained?

☐ yes   ☐ no

The seller should have the information on the tip of his or her tongue, even if only to say this maintenance work has never been done. Figure on at least $2500 to have the deferred maintenance done. Try to negotiate it as a discount on the purchase price.

What Brand of Paint Was Used?

☐ yes   ☐ no

If it was a high-quality brand, the seller will know. If the seller doesn't know and the home was recently repainted, chances are the painter used an off-brand (which will deteriorate sooner) to keep the price down. High-quality brands include Sherwin-Williams, Kelly-Moore, and Dunn Edwards, among others.

If Stucco, When Was a New Finish Coat Applied?

☐ yes   ☐ no

Theoretically, stucco should not be painted, but a new finish coat (which contains paint) should be applied. If a new finish coat was applied, expect the paint to look good for at least 10 years or longer. I have found that there is no problem in painting stucco.

Is a Home Owners' Association (HOA) Requiring a New Paint Coat?

☐ yes   ☐ no

Sometimes, if a home is part of a home owners association, the HOA may require that the house be repainted. Two reasons could be because the current paint is in bad condition, or even because the HOA did not approve the color originally used. If the owner is unsure, check with the HOA. Make sure the cost is deducted from the price of the home.

Do Any Neighbors Object to the Exterior Color or Look? ☐ yes ☐ no

You may want to think twice about buying into a neighborhood squabble. Are you willing to repaint to satisfy an irate neighbor? Will repainting even satisfy such a person?

Is There Any Deferred Maintenance? ☐ yes ☐ no

This is the broadest question. Carefully investigate any areas that the owner indicates need work.

Siding and Trim

SIDING—QUESTIONS TO ASK YOURSELF

If Metal, Is There Any Warping or Dents? ☐ yes ☐ no

Warping occurs because of a bad application. Dents occur when something strikes the metal, for example, falling branches. Usually warped or dented metal cannot be easily straightened, but must be replaced. The difficulty is finding similar siding. Replacement costs can be as little as $100 for a small area, but much more for an entire wall.

If Metal, Are There Any Rust Areas?   ☐ yes   ☐ no

Aluminum siding will not rust, but white oxidation can occur. Steel siding will rust if the paint covering wears off. Repainting may hide the stains, at least temporarily.

If Metal, Are There Any Wood Stains?   ☐ yes   ☐ no

These can occur when wood behind the siding gets wet and the water oozes out over the siding. The siding should be removed to determine if there's any wood rot and, if there is, the wood should be replaced before the siding is put back. A small wall can cost $500 to $1000 to repair.

If Metal, Are There Any Popped Nails?   ☐ yes   ☐ no

Popped nails usually occur when the wood behind the siding rots. Any popped nails should be taken seriously. If the nail slides in and out easily, it indicates bad wood behind. The siding should be removed and the wood examined and, if rotted, replaced. This usually occurs when the metal siding was not properly installed. A whole house replacement of both wood backing and siding can cost $5000 or more.

If Wood, Are There Any Soft Areas?   ☐ yes   ☐ no

Soft areas indicate rot behind the wood. The wood siding should be removed and examined. If rot is found, all contaminated wood should be replaced. The cost is determined by how big an area is involved. A small wall can easily cost $500 to remove, examine, and replace.

If Wood, Are There Any Unpainted Areas?

☐ yes ☐ no

Unpainted wood siding is subject to weathering. Within a few years the wood will deteriorate to the point where it no longer offers protection to the house. Sanding and painting can help cure the problem. Expect to pay about $3000 minimum for a good whole house painting.

If Wood, Is Any Mold Showing?

☐ yes ☐ no

Mold that is visible on the exterior of the siding may simply be surface growth, which can be brushed off, and the siding repainted with a fungus-resistant paint. However, if mold is coming from behind the siding, that indicates a more serious problem. If scraping reveals more mold, the siding should be removed and the backing examined.

If Vinyl, Are There Any Broken and/or Cracked Slats?

☐ yes ☐ no

Vinyl will last almost indefinitely, but will not hold up well to stress. If there is movement beneath the siding, the vinyl on the surface will express it often as cracks. Movement indicates a serious structural problem with the home. Have a structural engineer check it out.

TRIM—QUESTIONS TO ASK YOURSELF

Is Any Trim Missing?

☐ yes ☐ no

Missing trim is unsightly, but not usually a serious problem. Small pieces can usually be replaced quite easily and for a cost of under $50. The hard part is finding new trim to match the old.

Is There Any Nonconforming Trim?

☐ yes   ☐ no

Sometimes trim on one part of the house will not match that on another. This creates a hodge-podge look that detracts from the house value. All trim should match. A whole house replacement of trim can cost $500 to $1000 or more.

SIDING—QUESTIONS TO ASK SELLER-AGENT

Is the Siding Original?

☐ yes   ☐ no

If designed into the building of the home, and properly maintained, it should last indefinitely. If added later, be on the lookout for improper application and the possibility of water damage to the backing.

If Added, When Was the Work Done?

☐ yes   ☐ no

Recent work (less than three years ago) may not yet show any potential problems. If the work is older and there are still no signs of problems, it probably was done correctly.

If Added, Was It Done in the Summer or Winter?

☐ yes   ☐ no

Siding added during a dry summer is more likely to last longer. If done during the wet season when the backing was wet, that moisture may have been encapsulated and caused rotting.

TRIM—QUESTIONS TO ASK SELLER-AGENT

If Trim Is Nonconforming, Why? ☐ yes ☐ no

It could simply be that the homeowner was sloppy in maintenance. Or it could be that matching trim could not be found and the seller could not afford the cost of replacing all the trim on the home.

Porch and Deck

QUESTIONS TO ASK YOURSELF

Is the Porch and/or Deck in Proportion to the Home? ☐ yes ☐ no

The porch and/or deck should not overwhelm the home with its size. Nor should it be so small as to diminish the home's appearance. If not in proper proportion, a deck or porch can actually reduce the value of a property.

Is It Located in an Appropriate Area? ☐ yes ☐ no

Normally porches and/or decks are located at the back or sometimes the front of the home. There should be logical egress and ingress from a family room or living room, or a front door. Be wary if badly placed, for example, on the side of the house with the only access through a small bedroom. Inappropriate placement can knock down the value of the property.

Is It Covered?

☐ **yes**   ☐ **no**

A covered deck is worth much more than an uncovered one. Installing a deck covering can cost between $1500 and $5000, depending on size and type.

Does It Have Railings?

☐ **yes**   ☐ **no**

A good deck and/or porch will have railings about 3 feet high all along the periphery to help prevent anyone from falling off. Lack of railings can be a liability issue.

Are There Adequate Stairs?

☐ **yes**   ☐ **no**

Usually porches and decks connect to the ground (unless they are second-story or higher). Stairs should be at least 3 feet wide with railings and be properly anchored top and bottom. Narrow stairs or lack of railings can caused accidents, again a liability issue.

Is the Wood in Good Shape?

☐ **yes**   ☐ **no**

The wood should look fresh and solid. Wood that appears dried out, fragile, or otherwise deteriorated may indicate a worn-out or deteriorated deck or porch. Replacing the deck and/or porch wood can cost anywhere from $2500 on up, depending on size and materials used.

Are Any Nails Popping on the Deck?

☐ **yes**   ☐ **no**

Decking should be screwed down. If nails were used, they may pop up. These should be removed and screws put in their place. It's a tedious job, but you can do it in a few weekends. Popped nails can trip people walking on the deck and cause injuries.

Is There Any Warping?

☐ **yes**   ☐ **no**

Warped decking indicates improper construction. The decking should be screwed down to the support beams. If the decking is warped, there may not have been enough support or enough screws used.

Is There Any Sagging?

☐ **yes**   ☐ **no**

A deck and/or porch that visibly sags or gives when you walk on it has improper or damaged supports. Get a thorough inspection including estimates for replacement. Adding supports may solve the problem or the deck and/or porch may need to be rebuilt.

Is There Any Rotting?

☐ **yes**   ☐ **no**

Deck boards that are soft to the touch may indicate that support beams are rotting underneath. Also watch out for visible black mold. Any indication of rotting requires a thorough inspection. All rotted wood must be removed and replaced. Repair costs vary from a few hundred dollars to thousands to replace the entire structure.

Is There Good Spacing on Deck Boards?

☐ **yes**   ☐ **no**

Deck boards should have an air space of at least ⅛ to ¼ inch between them. This allows water to drain through and prevents rotting. Decks with no air space between boards were built incorrectly and are likely candidates for rotted wood.

Is the Deck Attached to the House?   ☐ yes   ☐ no

Ideally decks will come right up to a house, but will not be directly attached. The reason is that rot will frequently occur at the junction point. Many building departments, however, require house attachment for strength of the deck.

Was Metal Bracing Used?   ☐ yes   ☐ no

All support beams and joist junctions should have metal bracing. This adds immeasurably to the strength of the deck and/or porch.

Are There Cement Footings?   ☐ yes   ☐ no

The footings are where the deck and/or porch support beams contact the ground. Good footings are made of cement a foot square and are buried in the ground 18 inches or more. The wood support beam should be raised slightly off the cement and attached by a metal brace, to prevent termites from getting into the wood.

QUESTIONS TO ASK SELLER-AGENT

Was the Porch and/or Deck Original?   ☐ yes   ☐ no

If constructed as part of the home, you can feel fairly confident it was built to the code standards of the time. It should be professionally inspected, along with the house, of course.

If Added, Who Built It?

☐ **yes**   ☐ **no**

If a contractor built it, get the name. If it was the homeowner, be sure the professional home inspector pays special attention to the construction work.

If Added, Was It Built with a Permit?

☐ **yes**   ☐ **no**

Homeowners, and sometimes contractors, will add a porch and/or deck without the benefit of a building permit. The problem here is that it may not have been built to code and was not checked by a building inspector. The seller should be able to supply a copy of the permit or, if not, it will be on file at the county building department offices. You can ask the seller to bring the deck up to code before closing the deal.

Gutters

QUESTIONS TO ASK YOURSELF

Does the Home Have Gutters Throughout?

☐ **yes**   ☐ **no**

Whether or not a home has gutters is unlikely to affect its value to most buyers. However, by leading water away from the house, gutters help to ensure that over the years, there will be less chance of damage to the foundation.

Are the Gutters Wood, Metal, or Plastic?

☐ yes   ☐ no

Wood gutters are hardly ever used anymore, since they eventually rot out. Metal gutters last longer, particularly when they are anodized, but if made of steel, tend to eventually rust. Plastic gutters seem to last the longest and are rapidly becoming the most popular, partly because of ease of installation and lower cost.

Are There Downspouts?

☐ yes   ☐ no

Having gutters without downspouts is worse than having no gutters at all. The downspouts lead the water that the gutters collect down and away from the house.

Is the Water Directed Away from the Spouts?

☐ yes   ☐ no

Downspouts should send water away from the house. Often it is necessary to have cement splash basins or even plastic hoses leading the water away from the downspouts. In a well-thought-out system, the downspouts will often be connected to a French drain that leads water far away from the home.

Are the Gutters Clean?

☐ yes   ☐ no

Trees adjacent to the home often drop leaves on the roof that end up in the gutters. For most homes, gutters must be cleaned at least once a year. Plugged gutters not only are inefficient but the stagnant water they collect can be a breeding ground for insects such as mosquitoes.

Do They Sag?

☐ yes   ☐ no

Gutters that are in good shape will appear to follow the bottom line of the roof. Gutters that appear to sag have come loose and must be repaired. Typically this involves more than simply nailing them back—new sections must be attached. Figure from $100 to $1000 to fix sagging gutters.

Are There Any Broken Gutters?

☐ yes   ☐ no

Gutters with holes in them or that have broken off the roof, missing downspouts, and so on probably will need to be replaced, particularly if they are more than 10 years old. Figure around $1500 to $2500 for new gutters for an entire home.

If in Snow Country, Are the Gutters Below the Roofline?

☐ yes   ☐ no

Snow on the roof will accumulate, turn to ice during warming and cooling periods, and eventually rip off gutters that protrude beyond the roofline. Properly installed gutters in snow country will be below and slightly behind the roofline. Water will curl under the last shingle and drip off into them.

QUESTIONS TO ASK SELLER-AGENT

Did the Gutters Come with the House?

☐ yes   ☐ no

Gutters installed at the time the home was built speak of quality construction. It also suggests that they were probably built to code and approved by the building department.

If Added Later, How Long Ago?

☐ yes   ☐ no

Anytime longer than five years indicates that they should be inspected.

Who Installed Them?

☐ yes   ☐ no

Did the owner or a professional contractor install the gutters? If a contractor, does the owner have the name? If you're worried about the gutters, you can contact the contractor and ask about the work. Surprisingly, contractors often remember jobs and can comment knowledgeably about past work.

Why Were They Installed?

☐ yes   ☐ no

Gutters are rarely installed for cosmetic reasons. Ask if there was a water accumulation problem that necessitated gutters. Did the gutters relieve the problem, or does it still exist?

Are There Any Particular Problems with the Gutters?

☐ yes   ☐ no

Sometimes gutters lead to an underground drain system that must be cleaned periodically. Other times the system involves an electric sump pump that must be maintained. Sometimes a tree drops branches and leaves on a side of the house periodically damaging gutters. Find out what chronic problems may exist.

Roof

QUESTIONS TO ASK YOURSELF

What Kind of Roof Is It?

☐ yes   ☐ no

Different roofs have different life spans.

Type	Life Span, Years	Typical Cost
Tile, cement, or other masonry	50+	$15,000+
Metal (if not dented or scratched)	35+	$10,000+
Wood (depending on thickness)	15–30	$ 8,000+
Fiberglass and/or asphalt	10–25	$ 4,000+
Tar and gravel	7–25	$ 2,500+

Warning! Do not walk on masonry or metal roofs. If you do not know how to do so properly, you could easily and permanently damage the roof.

Are There Any Missing Shingles?

☐ yes   ☐ no

Missing shingles may allow the rain to get in. They must be replaced immediately to avoid ruining the underlayment (on masonry and wood roofs). The cost to replace a few missing shingles is under $100.

Is There Any Discoloration?

☐ yes   ☐ no

While not a major problem, discoloration looks bad and can adversely affect the value of the property. Usually the only way to remove the discoloration (except for wood) is to replace the roof. Wood roofs can be stained.

Are There Any Warped Shingles?

☐ yes   ☐ no

Shingles are warped if their ends curve upward. This is a particular problem with fiberglass or asphalt in very hot climates. Warping reduces the effectiveness of the shingles and shortens their life span. Usually it requires replacement of the entire roof.

Are Any Holes Visible?

☐ yes   ☐ no

There should never be any holes visible from the outside. If there are, get a complete roof inspection by a competent inspector. A complete reroofing may be necessary.

Is the Ridgeline Intact?

☐ yes   ☐ no

Wind will sometimes blow shingles off roof ridges. Replacement is simple and inexpensive. However, check for water damage inside, which could be extensive and costly to repair.

Is There Any Rusted Flashing?

☐ yes   ☐ no

Flashing is the metal around vents, chimneys, and so on. It is usually made of sheet metal and should be painted the color of the roof. Rusted flashing should be replaced before it leaks. Get a roofer to give you an estimate. Expect anywhere from $100 to $1000, depending on the extent of the work.

Is Any Light Visible from Inside the Attic?

☐ yes   ☐ no

On a bright day, go inside the attic and look up. If you see sparkles of light that look like stars, the roof has holes that will probably leak. It may require whole roof replacement.

Are There Any Water Stains in the Attic?

☐ yes   ☐ no

While you're in the attic, look for water stains on the wood supports. This indicates current or old leakage and should be checked out by a competent roofer.

Are There Any Water Stains on Ceilings?

☐ yes   ☐ no

Often water will run down roof rafters and supporting boards and stain ceilings. Check these out on the top floor of the house. If stains are present, look in the attic for additional water stains on rafters, joists, and beams. All suggest roof leakage, perhaps severe.

Are There Any Water Stains on Exterior Walls?   ☐ yes   ☐ no

Occasionally water from a leaking roof will wash down the outside of a house. This quickly stains the exterior. Water stains on the exterior should be treated as signs of a leaky roof, until another cause is discovered.

QUESTIONS TO ASK SELLER-AGENT

Does the Roof Leak?   ☐ yes   ☐ no

If the answer is yes, get an estimate of the cost to repair or replace the roof and negotiate to have the seller pay for it. If the seller says no, and there are signs of leakage, demand a thorough roof inspection.

Where Are the Leaks?   ☐ yes   ☐ no

A leak in the garage is not usually as worrisome as a leak over the living room. Some leaks, as over a patio, you can ignore. Leaks inside the house should be repaired prior to closing the deal.

How Old Is the Roof?   ☐ yes   ☐ no

Regardless of whether the roof is currently leaking, an old roof (see chart above) may only have a year or two of life left. Negotiate with the seller to have him or her pay at least part of the cost for a new roof.

Has the Roof Been Inspected Recently?　☐ **yes**　☐ **no**

If yes, ask to see the inspection report. Hiring your own inspector, however, even with an existing report, is always a good idea if you suspect any roof leakage.

Foundation (Exterior)

QUESTIONS TO ASK YOURSELF

Any Cracks Visible in the Foundation?　☐ **yes**　☐ **no**

Walk the perimeter of the home and look at the foundation. (It should be visible just below the siding.) Cracks should be easily discerned. Foundation repair is major work; even replacing a small portion can cost thousands. A whole house foundation repair can often cost $50,000 and much more. Unless you want a "fixer-upper," you are better off passing on a home with a bad foundation.

Are the Cracks "V"-Shaped?　☐ **yes**　☐ **no**

It is common to find tiny cracks in concrete. A crack that's larger at the top than at the bottom or is "V"-shaped indicates a break in the foundation and possibly in the reinforcement bars. It should be considered serious and investigated further by a structural engineer or a cement contractor.

Are There Any Offset Cracks?

☐ yes ☐ no

A crack where one side is higher than the other indicates a major ground shift that has stressed the foundation. It is a severe problem and may require replacement of at least a portion of the foundation.

Have Any Areas of the Foundation Been Recently Plastered and Painted?

☐ yes ☐ no

Normally the foundation is left bare or simply painted. Newly plastered and painted areas may conceal significant cracks. Ask the seller-agent about them.

Is There Any Standing Water Near the Foundation?

☐ yes ☐ no

All water should be led away from the house. Water standing near a foundation may eventually cause severe damage. Ask why the water was not directed away.

Any Large Trees and/or Tree Roots Near the Foundation?

☐ yes ☐ no

Large trees should be no nearer to the foundation than their drip line (the furthest extent of their branches). Anything closer can lead to roots traveling under the foundation and damaging it. Removal of a large tree can cost $500 and up, far cheaper than fixing a foundation.

Have Any Holes Been Punched Through the Foundation?

☐ yes   ☐ no

Sometimes workers will punch holes through a foundation for plumbing, electrical, or gas service. The proper way to handle this is to drill, but punching through with an automatic hammer is faster. Unfortunately, it usually cracks the concrete. If there are cracks around a punched hole, have your professional inspector give you an opinion as to whether or not it is serious.

QUESTIONS TO ASK SELLER-AGENT

Are There Any Problems with the Foundation?

☐ yes   ☐ no

The answer you expect should be no. If the seller says there is a problem, have it thoroughly evaluated by professionals. Sellers normally won't mention anything unless it's quite serious.

Has Any Corrective Work Ever Been Done to the Foundation?

☐ yes   ☐ no

Find out why this corrective work was done, who did it, and what they did. Call the contractor and find out if a building permit was issued. (It should have been.) Have your own professional inspector evaluate the work.

Are There Any Signs of Settling or Slippage of the Foundation?

☐ yes   ☐ no

These are the most serious problems, but are not always visible. If the seller indicates these problems, ask him or her to show you exactly where they are, so you can later point this out to an engineer or inspector.

Doors

QUESTIONS TO ASK YOURSELF

Is the Front Door Attractive?

☐ yes ☐ no

The front door(s) set the tone of the home. If they are richly wooded with fine brass handles, they say the house is high quality, expensive, and valuable. If they are cheap looking, they tell a different story. You'll pay more for a home with elegant doors . . . and you'll get more for one when you sell. A good front door begins at about $1200 installed and can easily cost $3000 or more.

Is There Any Visible Warping of the Doors? Do All Doors Close?

☐ yes ☐ no

This is a simple test: Swing the door shut. A properly hung door should close of its own weight. If it requires pressure to close, or if it doesn't close at all, it could be warped. Rehanging an interior door is inexpensive, under $100. Rehanging a front door can easily cost $300 or more. New hollow core interior doors cost as little as $50. Front doors start around $350 for the cheapest and go up to $5000 and more, depending on the materials used, installation extra.

Do All Door Locks Work?

☐ yes ☐ no

As a security measure, plan on changing the keying of all locks before you move in. You just want to be sure the current locks themselves are operative. Try locking the door to be sure the keys work.

Are There Doorstops Behind All Interior Doors?

☐ yes   ☐ no

A doorstop keeps the door from poking a hole in the wall behind it. All doors should have doorstops. Some are on the floor, others are on the wall, yet others are on the hinges. They are quite inexpensive (under $5), and fixing a hole can be a bothersome and time-consuming job.

Is the Front Door Handle Polished and Bright Looking?

☐ yes   ☐ no

Nothing says quality like a new-looking front door handle. If the existing handle is worn, it can cost upward of $250 or more to replace for a quality piece.

Is There a Dead Bolt on All Exterior Doors?

☐ yes   ☐ no

This is a necessity for security. Plan on spending between $50 and $100 per door to have them installed. You can do it yourself for just the cost of the dead bolt—around $35 for a good one.

Is There a Peep Hole on the Front Door?

☐ yes   ☐ no

A peep hole is a security feature that allows you to see who's at the door without opening it. The cost of the item is only around $5, but plan on spending $50 or more to have it professionally installed.

Are Any Doors Scratched or in Need of Paint or Stain?

☐ yes   ☐ no

Scratches on painted doors can usually be filled and then repainted. Scratches on stained doors are more difficult. They must usually be sanded (sometimes this is not possible if the door has a thin veneer of wood) and then the entire door stained to match. Scratches on metal doors must be filled and sanded before the entire door can be repainted. The cost can be several hundred dollars. Sometimes it's cheaper to simply replace the door.

Is There a Fire Door Between the Garage and House?

☐ yes   ☐ no

Fires occasionally start in garages where paints and other chemicals may be stored. A solid core fire door between the house and the garage is a must. To buy and install, figure around $200 or more.

Does the Garage-to-House Door Close Automatically?

☐ yes   ☐ no

To prevent auto exhaust fumes from getting into the house, the door should close by itself. Auto closers cost around $20 and are easily installed.

Is There Weather Stripping on All Exterior Doors?

☐ yes   ☐ no

In these days of high energy costs, all doors should be properly weather-stripped. The cost of the stripping is relatively low (under $25 a door), but installation can be tricky. Plan on spending $50 a door to have it properly installed.

Do All Sliders Work Smoothly?

☐ yes   ☐ no

Rollers on glass sliding doors can rust, crack, or simply disintegrate over time. This will be evident if the door is difficult to slide open or closed. Sometimes the rollers can be replaced (cost is under $5), although paying for replacement can cost $50. Other times, the entire sliding glass window and sometimes the entire assembly including casing must be replaced. Figure $1000 for a sliding glass door replacement, including labor.

Are All Sliders Safety Glass?

☐ yes   ☐ no

Virtually all sliding glass doors sold today are some type of safety glass. However, sliders in older homes may not be. Look for the safety glass emblem, which can usually be found in a corner of the glass. A slider can break and if it's not safety glass, large shards of glass can seriously injure anyone nearby.

Do All Exterior Gate Doors Work? Do They Automatically Close?

☐ yes   ☐ no

Outside gate doors should swing back and close on their own. (You can put a lock on a gate door to secure it completely.) Sometimes, however, they tilt or warp and don't close well. Often the cause is a tilted post, which may be corrected with just a few minutes of work. Other times, however, the post or even the entire gate may need to be replaced. Figure on $100 minimum for exterior gate door replacement, more if it's metal.

QUESTIONS TO ASK SELLER-AGENT

Were Any Doors Recently Replaced? Why?

☐ yes   ☐ no

Doors may be replaced as a simple upgrading of the property, or because they were symptomatic of a more serious problem, such as foundation or structural cracking or slipping. Find out why the doors were replaced.

Are There Any Problems with Doors?

☐ yes   ☐ no

Find out if any doors currently do not work properly or have other problems. Check them out. Determine what the problem is and how costly it will be to replace or repair.

Are There Any Weather-Stripping Door Problems?

☐ yes   ☐ no

Is the weather stripping missing, or is it damaged or ineffective? Doing it yourself can cost less than $100. Having it done by an expert may require door replacement and can be quite costly.

Windows

QUESTIONS TO ASK YOURSELF

Are There Any Broken Windows?

☐ yes   ☐ no

Walk around the house. Very quickly you'll discover if any of the windows are broken. Insist that the seller fix all broken windows prior to the close of escrow. (The cost can be anywhere from around $75 a window on up to over $1000, depending on whether they are double-pane, special cut, safety glass, and so on, and also depending on their size and how difficult it would be to access them.)

Are There Any Broken Window Screens?

☐ yes   ☐ no

All windows that open should have screens. And the screens should be in good condition—no tears, rips, or holes. Broken screens may seem like a minor matter, but can easily cost $25 a window or more for rescreening. Have the seller fix any broken screens.

Are All Windows Double-Pane?

☐ yes   ☐ no

At one time double-pane windows, renowned for their insulating abilities, were the exception. Today they are found everywhere, even in areas of the country with moderate temperatures. A house with double-pane windows is more desirable than one without them, and often commands a higher price. The cost for inexpensive Milgard (one of the top manufacturers) retrofits starts at about $200 and up per window, depending on size and type, plus the cost of installation.

Do Windows Have "low-e" Ratings?

☐ yes   ☐ no

This refers to a special coating that is applied to double-pane windows that can double or even quadruple their insulating qualities. A low-e window can have an r-7 rating, compared to r-2 for double-pane and r-1 for single-pane. It costs around $2 per square foot to add this to windows. It can only be done in the manufacturing stage, not after they're installed. Upgrading all the glass on an average house will cost around $8000.

Do All Sliders Have Safety Glass?

☐ yes   ☐ no

Slider can break when someone accidentally walks into them, closes them too hard, or hits them with a heavy object. Again, the shards of regular glass are extremely dangerous. Check in the corners of the slider glass for a safety glass label. Safety glass replacements cost between $500 and $1000 for inexpensive sliders.

Are There Any Water Stains Around Windows?

☐ yes   ☐ no

Water stains suggest leaks. Water may be coming in because the windows don't fit well. Or there may be leaks around the outside edges of the windows, suggesting improper installation. Get a glazier to give you a cost estimate and have the seller pay for window repairs.

Is There Any Rust Around Windows?

☐ yes   ☐ no

This usually occurs only with older steel windows. Sometimes there is rust simply because the paint coat has deteriorated, allowing water to touch the metal. Scraping, sanding, and repainting should fix it. Check to make sure the rust doesn't signal a leak in the window (see above).

QUESTIONS TO ASK SELLER-AGENT

Were Any Windows Replaced? Why?

☐ yes　　☐ no

It's very costly to replace windows, typically from $4000 to $8000 and up for an entire house. Find out why the owner did it. Was it to upgrade and for better insulation? Was it because of leaking? If leaks, were all the problems corrected?

Are There Any Weather-Stripping Problems with Windows?

☐ yes　　☐ no

Check for windows that would let in rain, wind, or cold. Look for windows that don't close fully, or that don't fit in their frame properly. The weather stripping will need to be fixed or replaced. In some instances, the entire window will need to be replaced.

Garbage Can Space

QUESTIONS TO ASK YOURSELF

Is There a Space Dedicated to the Garbage Cans?

☐ yes　　☐ no

You want garbage cans out of sight and out of mind. That means a space, usually at the side of the house, where they can be kept unobtrusively. You will always regret owning a home where the cans must be kept in sight in the yard or take up space in the garage. Check to see if you can build a storage location.

Is It Easily Accessible to the Front of the House?

☐ yes   ☐ no

Today in most areas, you must haul the can to the street for pickup. Is there easy access from the garbage can storage area to the front yard? If cans have to be hauled through the home they can cause a mess on carpets and leave unpleasant odors in the home.

Are the Garbage Cans Stored Near a Window Where Odors Can Get into the House?

☐ yes   ☐ no

You don't want to be forced to keep a window permanently closed because the garbage cans are beneath it. Is there an alternative holding area?

How Many Cans Does It Hold?

☐ yes   ☐ no

Today many areas require the use of three separate garbage cans. One for trash, another for green cuttings, and yet another for recyclables. Is there room for all?

Is the Holding Area an Eyesore?

☐ yes   ☐ no

This can be a downer for the entire neighborhood, if everyone's garbage cans are out front. Remember that you might be able to change the location of your own garbage can storage, but you can't easily change your neighbors'.

QUESTIONS TO ASK SELLER-AGENT

Is There Regular Garbage Collection? How Often?

☐ yes ☐ no

Almost all incorporated areas have service. Many rural areas do not. Where there's no service, you have to haul the garbage to the dump yourself. Ask what the service (or the dump) costs are as well as how often are the pickups.

Do You Have to Put the Can on the Street?

☐ yes ☐ no

It's a lot easier if the garbage collectors will come to the can, rather than the other way around. If you have to haul the cans out yourself, is there a neighborhood requirement (enforced by the home owners' association) that you must not put the cans out before a certain hour and must have them in by a certain time? If so, can you live with this bother?

Are There Separate Pickups for "Green" Refuse and Recyclables?

☐ yes ☐ no

The seller will know. Also, find out if there's a reduced fee if you separate recyclables or don't have a green can.

Rubbish Accumulation

QUESTIONS TO ASK YOURSELF

Is There Any Rubbish Around the House?

☐ yes   ☐ no

Some owners are punctilious about keeping the areas around their home clean and clear. Others let all sorts of trash accumulate over the years. Walk around the home and observe any trash—insist that it be fully removed prior to close of escrow; otherwise, you'll have the sometimes difficult job of hauling it off yourself.

Is It Permanent or Temporary?

☐ yes   ☐ no

If it's just debris, it can usually be hauled away easily. Sometimes, however, the debris consists of part of concrete foundations, pipes in the ground, leftover paint, or other toxic chemicals. All these items may require heavy work, specialized disposal, or even permits to have them removed. Be sure you make this rubbish problem the seller's responsibility, not yours.

If Rubbish is on the Sides of the House, Does It Block Water Runoff?

☐ yes   ☐ no

Often rubbish is allowed to accumulated on the side of the home blocking the natural runoff of water. If so, check for water accumulation and damage. Sometimes the trash is the minor problem, and the water damage is the more serious concern.

If the Rubbish Is in Front of the House, Does It Affect Appearance? ☐ yes ☐ no

If there's rubbish in front of the house, it can decrease the value of the home, perhaps allowing you to buy it for less. You can then remove the trash and have a more valuable home. If there's rubbish in the front of neighboring houses, however, there's little you can do about it, and it will continue to affect the price of the home you buy.

QUESTIONS TO ASK SELLER-AGENT

Will You Remove All Rubbish before Close of Escrow? ☐ yes ☐ no

If the answer is no, ask why not? Is there a toxic waste problem? If so, reconsider your purchase. It can cost tens of thousands of dollars to remove such items. Is the seller just stubborn or lazy by not getting rid of the rubbish? Negotiate harder to get your way.

Why Is the Rubbish There? ☐ yes ☐ no

The assumption is that the rubbish is there because of a careless seller. This is not always the case. The rubbish may be concealing a serious defect. Specify that you have the right to inspect and approve the property *after* all rubbish has been removed.

3
The Foundation

Foundations and Slabs

QUESTIONS TO ASK YOURSELF

Can You Easily See the Foundation from the Inside? ☐ yes ☐ no

From the outside, the foundation is usually quite easy to see. From the inside, however, unless there's a basement or access room, it's more difficult. (Chances are, you won't want to go into a low crawl space under the house.) The following questions apply *if* you can easily see the foundation.

How Thick Is It?

☐ yes   ☐ no

It should be thicker than the mudsill (the board that lays on top of it) by at least an inch on either side. If the board is 6 inches wide, the foundation should be 8 inches wide. If the board is 4 inches, the foundation should be at least 6 inches. (Note: A 2×4 is actually only 3.5 inches wide; a 2×6 is actually only 5.5 inches wide.) A narrower foundation may not be strong enough to support the house over a long period of time.

Is It Concrete?

☐ yes   ☐ no

Modern foundations are primarily poured concrete. Concrete blocks can be used, but are not considered as strong. Stone and brick foundations, found in older homes, can slip, particularly in earthquakes or high winds.

Is It *in* the Ground or *on* the Ground?

☐ yes   ☐ no

An important difference: "In the ground" means the bulk of the foundation is actually buried below ground level—structurally sound. "On the ground" means that a mudsill (typically a piece of redwood) was laid on mud and the foundation built on top of it—unsound and found only in older homes). For safety reasons, a mudsill foundation on the ground should be replaced—the cost is often $50,000 and up.

If the Foundation Is on a Slope, Is It Stepped?

☐ yes   ☐ no

A simple foundation on a slope simply follows the slope and is higher at the low end. A "stepped" foundation has steps that go down the slope and has many levels. Of the two, a stepped foundation is far stronger.

Is Any Slippage Evident?

☐ **yes** ☐ **no**

This is usually quite easy to see. The foundation will be twisted; there could be holes under it, and dirt could be coming through from outside. Have a contractor and a soils engineer check any slippage at all but beware—the cost to fix it can be more than the house itself is worth!

Are There Any Significant Cracks?

☐ **yes** ☐ **no**

A crack is significant if it is more than $\frac{1}{16}$ inch thick and is wider at the top than at the bottom. It indicates a broken foundation. Over time, the crack could widen and cause severe damage to the house. This is particularly the case in freezing climates or where there is ground movement.

Is There Any Standing Water?

☐ **yes** ☐ **no**

There should never be water puddles near the foundation, as this could undermine it. Drains may have to be installed to carry standing water off. Get a contractor to give you an estimate and have the seller pay for all or at least a significant part of the work.

Are There Any Watermarks?

☐ **yes** ☐ **no**

These can be seen as either dark gray or sometimes white phosphorescent marks on the foundation. Watermarks indicate that, at some time in the past, water has risen above the ground. The big questions are What caused it? and Will it happen again? Get a professional inspector's opinion.

Are There Any Air Gaps between the Foundation and the Sill?   ☐ yes   ☐ no

These are caused either by poor construction or by later slippage. The wood sill should be tight to the foundation. Get a contractor to give you an opinion as to why there are gaps and how to correct the problem.

QUESTIONS TO ASK SELLER-AGENT

Are There Any Problems with the Foundation?   ☐ yes   ☐ no

The seller should know and should disclose this information. If the seller says there are none, get it in writing. This will help you later on if it develops that there were problems. Investigate thoroughly any problems the seller discloses.

Has Anyone Advised You to Have the Foundation Fixed?   ☐ yes   ☐ no

This slightly different phrasing can be important. A building inspector, contractor, or other inspector may have told the seller there was a problem, even though the seller didn't believe it. Get a copy of the report.

Did You Build This House?   ☐ yes   ☐ no

If the seller built the home, he or she should be able to give you additional valuable information (below) about the foundation. If not, this information should be available from the local building department, should you care to investigate.

Was Rebar Used in the Foundation?

☐ yes   ☐ no

This refers to steel reinforcement bars that should always be used. Don't assume they were! Some contractors leave them out. This usually means the foundation will eventually fail. It's almost impossible to tell just by looking.

How Deep Are the Footings?

☐ yes   ☐ no

This refers to how far below ground level the foundation goes. In mild climates with good gravel soil, the footings need not be more than 12 inches deep. In areas where there is ground slippage or expansion, 18 inches to 2 feet is often considered minimum. In freezing climates it should be below the frost line, often 40 or more inches deep. A too-small footing will result in the eventual cracking of the foundation.

The Foundation Supports

QUESTIONS TO ASK YOURSELF

Are There Piers under the House?

☐ yes   ☐ no

In addition to a peripheral foundation, most homes also have piers that support the floor joists under the home. These are typically made of wood (perhaps 6 × 8) with cement footers underneath and floor joists on top. They support the bottom floor and sometimes structurally help support the upper floors and roof. It's important that they be sound and in good condition.

Do You Have Easy Access?

☐ yes ☐ no

Often, homes have a basement or, barring that, an access door so that you can easily see the piers. If you cannot, you will eventually want to hire a professional to root around under the house in narrow crawl spaces to check them out.

Are the Piers on Cement Footers?

☐ yes ☐ no

The last thing you want to see are piers anchored directly to the ground. These will soon rot out, if the termites don't get them first. Retrofitting mudsill piers with cement, because of the difficulty in getting to the area, can cost many thousands of dollars, even for just a few piers.

Are Any Piers Leaning, Bowing, or Cracking?

☐ yes ☐ no

The wood piers should be standing straight up and should look just as fresh as the day they were installed. In an adequately ventilated space, they will age very slowly and can continue to support the home for well over 50 years (perhaps over 100!). Any bowing, cracking, or aging indicates a problem that should be examined by a structural engineer.

Are There Any Watermarks?

☐ yes ☐ no

This indicates a high water level sometime in the past. If you see these marks, or if the piers are in standing water, have a soils engineer check it out. It could require installation of a drain system (anywhere from $500 to $5000, depending on complexity).

Has There Been Any Earthquake Retrofitting?

☐ yes ☐ no

Heavy metal braces running from the cement footings to the joists at the top of the piers are usually earthquake retrofits, designed to keep the home from moving in a temblor. These are expensive to install and their existence indicates that someone has gone to extra effort to protect the home.

Are the Connectors Made of Metal?

☐ yes ☐ no

Ideally, the wood piers will be attached to the joists at the top with a metal cap that nails on to both. At the bottom, the piers will be attached by a metal connector that is sunk into the concrete. This adds enormously to their strength (they won't fall apart in an earthquake or heavy wind-storm) and acts to keep termites from traveling up the piers into the home.

QUESTIONS TO ASK SELLER-AGENT

Are There Any Problems with the Foundation Supports?

☐ yes ☐ no

If the seller doesn't know what you're talking about, it's a good sign. If the seller readily admits there have been problems, ask for reports, invoices, and other documentation and have it thoroughly checked out.

Have There Been Any Changes, Supports Added, or New Joists?

☐ yes ☐ no

New work suggests a problem. Find out what the problem was and what was done to correct it. Have a professional evaluate the work. If the seller did it him- or herself, the solution could be worse than the problem!

The Slab

QUESTIONS TO ASK YOURSELF

What Is a "Slab"?

☐ yes   ☐ no

In many homes, from inexpensive to the most luxurious, the floor is concrete poured to a minimum depth of 4 inches and called a *slab*. A nonpermeable membrane (plastic) must be placed between the ground and the slab to prevent moisture from coming through. In addition, rebars (reinforcement steel bars) must be placed in the slab to keep it from moving and from cracking.

How Do I Know if the House Has a Slab?

☐ yes   ☐ no

If the home has wall-to-wall carpeting on the first floor, *with the owner's permission*, peel back a corner. Peel back some of the padding underneath, and you'll immediately see if the floor is concrete or wood.

Is the Slab Cracked?

☐ yes   ☐ no

The biggest problem with slabs is cracking. Minor cracks are to be expected. Big cracks, particularly where one side is offset against the other, are a serious problem. If the slab is underneath tile or linoleum, the crack will often show through. Under carpeting you can sometimes see it by getting down low and looking for an unusual cross-room shadow. You can usually detect slab cracks by taking off your shoes and walking over the suspected area; you'll feel it underfoot.

Is the Crack Serious?

☐ yes   ☐ no

If the crack indicates continuing movement, it should be considered serious. If it indicates old movement that's stopped, it can probably be dealt with cosmetically. A cosmetic treatment usually means sanding down the offset and patching—at a cost of several hundred dollars. Replacing a broken slab usually starts at around $10,000 per room. Have a soils engineer and a cement contractor look at it.

Is There a Standing Water Problem?

☐ yes   ☐ no

Usually slabs crack because of ground water rising up underneath. Sometimes a drain can be installed around the periphery of the house to lead water away. This may stabilize the slab, allowing cosmetic repair. Check for standing water at the rear and sides of the house. Get a soils report.

Is the Slab Wet?

☐ yes   ☐ no

The surface of the slab should never be wet. If it is, the moisture will usually come right through flooring such as carpeting or tiles and be evident in the form of moisture and mold. This suggests that the necessary impermeable membrane was never placed beneath the slab, the membrane is damaged, or there is a high water table. In all cases, it is a very serious problem and requires further inspection as noted above. Keep in mind that solving this may require replacing the slab. Or there may be no solution economically possible!

Are the Rebars Missing or Broken? ☐ yes ☐ no

The only way you'll know is if there's a big crack (more than ¼ inch wide) and you can look down into it. If you don't see steel bars holding the two sides together, chances are they were never placed in the slab. The only sure remedy is to replace the slab. If there is a significant offset between the two sides of a crack, the slab should be replaced.

QUESTIONS TO ASK SELLER-AGENT

Are There Any Cracks in the Slab? ☐ yes ☐ no

If it's covered with carpeting, the seller may not know. If the seller indicates there are, then suspect a significant problem and have it checked out, as indicated above.

Are There Rebars in the Slab? ☐ yes ☐ no

Often it's not just one house that has this problem, but the whole tract of houses in which the builder cheated. The seller may be able to tell you if this is a common problem. If you're suspicious, also check with the local building department.

Are There Any Water Problems with the Slab? ☐ yes ☐ no

If there are, most sellers will admit it. After all, it will be pretty evident after a good rainfall. Have the problem analyzed and be prepared to pass on the house if it's serious.

Were There Any Attempts to Fix the Slab?

☐ yes   ☐ no

What was done? Was a new slab poured with rebar in it and was a membrane installed? Was the original slab first removed? Check with a contractor to see if the work was done appropriately and what the chances are of the problem recurring.

4

Infrastructure

Plumbing and Pipes

QUESTIONS TO ASK YOURSELF

Are the Pipes Galvanized Iron?

☐ **yes**   ☐ **no**

Galvanized iron was used for years as the primary water piping in homes in the United States. You can tell by checking the pipes as they enter the house or above the water heater where they enter the wall. Galvanized pipe is gray in color. If the pipe is painted, scratch on it gently with a screwdriver or key and the true color will show through. The life span of galvanized pipe is around 35 to 50 years in most areas. After that, rusting will cause leaks, and the pipes must be replaced.

Are the Pipes Copper?

☐ yes   ☐ no

Modern homes use copper piping. It is more expensive than galvanized, but easier to install and it has fewer problems. The life span is almost indefinite. At the water heater or where water pipes enter the home, scratch the pipe gently. It should be a bright, copper color.

Are the Pipes PVC?

☐ yes   ☐ no

PVC is often used to bring potable water from the street to the house and for irrigation systems. Only a few cities allow it to be used throughout the home. The reason is that it is more easily damaged or broken, resulting in leaks. It can last almost indefinitely, and it is easy to install. There are some health concerns about leaching of toxic chemicals from the pipe into the water system.

Are There Any Visible Leaks?

☐ yes   ☐ no

Water stains or wet walls are signs of leaks. Any leak in an old galvanized pipe system suggests that the piping is wearing out and must be replaced. It costs around $7500 to replace piping in an average-size house, plus the cost of repairing damage to walls caused by the repairs. Leaks to galvanized pipes can be temporarily fixed by using pressure clamps. Leaks in copper and PVC are easily, quickly, and permanently repaired. Figure a minimum of several hundred dollars for a plumber to fix a leak.

Are There Antisiphon Valves on the Sprinkler System?

☐ yes ☐ no

Antisiphon valves prevent polluted water from siphoning back into the home's potable water system. They should be installed *above the level of the highest sprinkler head* on all irrigation systems. They cost around $20 apiece (electrically operated), but installation can run around $50 apiece.

Is There a Pressure Control Valve in Front of the House?

☐ yes ☐ no

For areas with high water pressure, this is a valve that goes on the water line just before it enters the home. It costs about $80, plus another $100 or so to have it installed. High water pressure at the taps suggests that the valve is missing or not working properly. A professional inspector can measure the water pressure in the home to determine if there's a problem.

QUESTIONS TO ASK SELLER-AGENT

Have There Been Any Leaks? Where? How Were They Fixed?

☐ yes ☐ no

Occasional leaks in PVC and copper piping are to be expected, especially in freezing weather. Leaks to galvanized piping, as noted above, can be serious. If the seller says pressure clamps were applied, it is possible that all the galvanized pipe in the home may need to be replaced. The seller should pay all or most of this cost.

Were Any Pipes Replaced? Why? Who Did the Work?

☐ yes ☐ no

If a whole or partial pipe replacement was done, ask why? Was all the galvanized pipe removed, or only a portion? (All is better.) Did a professional do it? Ask to see an estimate and the invoice and, if there are concerns, call the plumber.

Heating and Furnace

QUESTIONS TO ASK YOURSELF

Are the Vents High or Low?

☐ yes ☐ no

The location of vents helps determine circulation patterns. Vents placed low in walls or floors work best with heating, since hot air rises. Vents placed high in walls or ceilings work best with air-conditioning. On the other hand, high heating vents mean that the floor area will never fully warm up. Low air-conditioning vents mean that the air at the top of rooms will never fully cool off. Ideally, there would be separate vents for heating and cooling, but to save money in construction that almost never happens.

Are There Ceiling Fans?

☐ yes ☐ no

These can mitigate the bad effects of misplaced vents. Fans cost anywhere from $50 to $1000, depending on quality and features. (More expensive fans make less noise, have more speeds, and are remotely controlled.) Installation, including running electrical wiring, can cost another $200 to $400.

Are Any Vents Blocked? Do All Vents Work?

☐ yes ☐ no

Make sure that all vents open and close easily. With the furnace on, put your hand in front of each vent in the home. You should feel a strong blast of air. If no air comes through a vent, it's probably blocked. You'll need to call a furnace service to check it out.

Is the Filter Clean?

☐ yes ☐ no

Usually it's quite easy to open the furnace door and check the filter. Dirty filters reduce heating and cooling efficiency. They cost under $15 to replace.

Is the Fan Making Any Squeaky Noises?

☐ yes ☐ no

Squeaks mean that the fan motor's bearings are running dry. Unfortunately, most fan motors in heaters are permanently sealed. That means that when the bearings run dry, you can't oil or replace them. Rather, you need to replace the whole motor—typically around $250 and up, including labor.

Does the Heater Go On when You Turn Up the Thermostat?

☐ yes   ☐ no

If it's forced air, there's usually a few minutes' delay. The burners first come on and then, after the air has heated up a bit, the fan motor (which is what you hear) comes on. With radiated heat you will often only be able to tell by creaks and groans from the radiators. Wait about 15 minutes and then check the vents or radiators for warmth. If there's no heat, have a heating service check it out. Replacing a heating system can easily cost $2500 and more. Have the seller pay for it.

How Old Is the Unit?

☐ yes   ☐ no

Furnaces will normally have a plate on them that gives you the date of manufacture. Over the last 10 years the efficiency of heaters has increased enormously. You can estimate that a 10-year-old (or older) furnace will cost you nearly twice as much in fuel as a brand-new one. You may want to think about replacing an old furnace—this is not something the seller will usually agree to pay for.

Does It Offer Regional Controls?

☐ yes   ☐ no

With water and/or radiator heaters, you often can control regions of the home, warming some while leaving others cooler. With forced air, this is sometimes possible through baffles in the ducting. A heating system with regional control is much better, since you only need to heat the area in which you are living and can thus save on fuel costs.

Are There Vents and/or Radiator Grills around the Periphery and Under Windows?

☐ yes ☐ no

The vents or grills should be located around the periphery of the home for greatest efficiency. The best locations are near doors and under windows where there is most likely to be the greatest amount of heat transfer. Relocating badly placed vents in a completed structure is expensive, sometimes costing $1000 or more.

Are There Any Leaks in the Water System?

☐ yes ☐ no

Water and/or radiant heating systems sometimes have radiators; other times they have coils in the floor or ceiling. Unfortunately, these can start to leak through normal house settling. If the coils can be reached, they can readily be fixed. However, if the coil that breaks is located in a cement slab, it may be simpler and cheaper to install a completely new system. A break in a ceiling coil can ruin a room full of furniture or worse. Look for telltale watermarks. Once a system has leaked, the chances are great that it will leak again.

Are There Any Leaks in the Oil System?

☐ yes ☐ no

Oil heaters usually have a storage tank, often in the basement. Leaks from the tank can produce odors and can damage flooring. Typically, you can detect these types of problems just by looking. Have the seller correct any problems.

Is There Easy Access to the Filter and the Furnace?

☐ yes ☐ no

You'll want to change the filter every month when the furnace is being used. Having easy access to the filter helps here. Some furnaces located in attic spaces are difficult to work on and require a professional's aid even just to change the filter. It can cost $50 to $100 every time you call someone out.

Do All Burners Work? Are the Flames Yellow or Blue?

☐ yes ☐ no

It takes an expert to determine if a furnace is working correctly. However, if you can see the flames when the furnace is on without opening the door, look for blue flames. That usually means the gas is fully combusted. The furnace needs servicing if you see yellow flames or if some burners are not working. Make sure the seller pays for this servicing.

Is the Heat Exchanger Okay?

☐ yes ☐ no

The heat exchanger is a metal barrier—dangerous exhaust fumes escape on one side, warm air is circulated through the house on the other. Any holes will let dangerous fumes into the house. Have a professional inspector check this out. About the only way you, yourself, can tell if there are fumes is if a carbon monoxide detector in the home is showing high readings.

Is the Thermostat Operative? Does It Have Conservation Features?
☐ yes   ☐ no

Check the thermostat by turning it up high and then down low. The furnace should respond by going on and off. There should also be a separate switch that operates just the fan. A good thermostat will offer conservation features such as a setback for nighttime. Modern digital thermostats offer as many as half a dozen different settings for each day of the week so you can determine precisely when you want the heat to come on and go off. They cost under $100.

Is the Gas Service Adequate?
☐ yes   ☐ no

If you're using natural gas, it's important that the line coming in from outside is thick enough to service all of the home's needs. Usually a ¾-inch line is sufficient for a gas heater and water heater. But if there is also a gas dryer and a fireplace insert, then the line should be at least 1 inch in diameter. Upgrading the gas line within the house requires the services of a professional and can easily cost several thousand dollars. If a bigger line is required to bring in gas to the house from the street, it might be paid for by the gas company.

QUESTIONS TO ASK SELLER-AGENT

Are There Any Problems with the Heating System?
☐ yes   ☐ no

This is one of those catch-all questions. If the answer is no, get it in writing. If yes, find out exactly what the problem was, how it was remedied, and by whom. Then have a professional check it out to be sure it was done properly.

When Was the Last Time the Furnace Was Serviced? How Was the Problem Solved?

☐ yes   ☐ no

An old furnace usually needs frequent servicing. If it hasn't been serviced in a long time, it may just be a matter of time before it breaks. Find out what items were replaced at the last servicing since, hopefully, these won't need replacing for a long time to come.

How Long Does It Take to Heat the Home?

☐ yes   ☐ no

A good forced-air furnace should be able to easily raise the temperature in the home 20 degrees in an hour. If the owner says it takes several hours, the furnace may be too small for the house. Have a furnace professional check it out, then negotiate with the owner about a replacement.

Is There Any Warranty on the Heater?

☐ yes   ☐ no

Don't expect a warranty on older furnaces. However, furnaces under 10 years of age may have some warranty left. In addition, a home warranty plan put on the home as part of the sale may cover some (but usually not all) of the cost of furnace repair or replacement.

Electrical

QUESTIONS TO ASK YOURSELF

Is It Safe for You to Check the Electrical System?

☐ yes   ☐ no

Unless you're competent with home electrical systems, leave this entirely to a professional. Do *not* stick anything into any plugs. Do not stick your hand into a circuit breaker box.

Are There Adequate Plugs in Every Room?

☐ yes   ☐ no

There should be a receptacle about every 12 feet. That usually means at least one in every wall. If there is no ceiling light, the wall switch should control at least one of the receptacles. Rewiring to add more plugs can cost hundreds if not thousands of dollars.

Are Plugs and Switches Stylish and a Modern Color?

☐ yes   ☐ no

At one time, all switches, plugs, and cover plates were ivory or a dark brown. Now there are many shades of white and other colors. Additionally, there are many styles, from sliders to throw switches. Basic switches, plugs, and plates are very inexpensive, costing only a few dollars. Stylish units cost far more, often $10 to $30 per unit, uninstalled.

Is the Electrical Service Big Enough?

☐ yes ☐ no

A modern home with washer and/or dryer, kitchen appliances, furnace, and so on needs at least a 200-amp circuit. Anything less will be inadequate. Older homes sometimes only have 100-amp or even just 60-amp service. Bringing in a more powerful service will cost thousands, depending on how much work must be done. The amperage will usually be shown on the circuit breaker box.

Does the Home Have Circuit Breakers?

☐ yes ☐ no

All modern homes do. Many older homes still use fuses. Test the circuit breakers by flipping them off *all the way,* then resetting them. If they won't reset, they should be replaced. Have an electrician do it. The cost is about $10 to $25 per breaker, plus a hundred dollars or so for the electrician.

Do the Kitchen and Utility Room Have 220-V Service?

☐ yes ☐ no

An electric range or electric clothes dryer requires 220-V service. You can usually tell 220-V from 110-V service by the large round receptacle in the wall with three large openings in it. Do NOT put anything into the openings to test it. A home inspector can quickly tell by using a voltmeter. Wiring a kitchen and utility room for 220 V can cost anywhere from $500 to $1500. Most sellers will not pay for this.

QUESTIONS TO ASK SELLER-AGENT

Are There Any Electrical Problems?

☐ yes ☐ no

If the answer is no, get it in writing. If the answer is yes, find out exactly what the problem is and get an electrical contractor to give you an estimate on having it fixed. Have the seller absorb the costs.

Air-Conditioning

QUESTIONS TO ASK YOURSELF

Does Cool Air Blow Out?

☐ yes ☐ no

The standard method of testing an air-conditioning system is to use two thermometers, one in the air intake to the blower and the other in a vent. If the differential temperature is 4 to 6 degrees, the system is working. You can do roughly the same thing by turning on the air and putting your hand to a vent. Cold (not cool) air should blow out. If it doesn't, the system may not be working.

Are There Any Leaks?

☐ yes ☐ no

Only a professional can tell for sure, but if you look at the lines connecting to the compressor and they seem loose and the system isn't blowing cold air, there could be a leak. Have it checked out. Fixing a system can cost as little as $100 or as much as $2500, depending on what's wrong.

Are Any Lines Sweating?

☐ yes   ☐ no

When the air conditioner is turned on, any moisture on the lines that come out of the compressor suggests that the system is not fully operative. Have it checked by a professional.

How Old Is the System?

☐ yes   ☐ no

Air conditioners have improved enormously over the past few years. A brand-new system is likely to be three times more efficient than one that is only 10 years old. The newer the system, the less (far less) it will cost you to operate it.

Are the Vents Located High or Low on the Walls?

☐ yes   ☐ no

Vents located high on the walls are best for air-conditioning. (Hot air rises causing cooler air to fall, thus creating circulation in the room.) Be sure there's an air-conditioning vent in every room. Rooms without vents will not be cooled.

Are There Individual Window Units?

☐ yes   ☐ no

Depending on size (measured in BTUs), these can easily cool an entire room. Figure a minimum of about 10,000 BTUs for an average-size room. However, having half a dozen individual units will use many times more electricity than one central unit.

Does the Compressor Make a Lot of Noise? Is This Bothersome? ☐ yes ☐ no

Newer units are whisper silent. As units age, they can get noisy. A squeal indicates a fan motor is about to die. A low rumble suggests problems with the compressor. A fan can cost several hundred dollars to replace. A compressor unit can easily cost $1000. Have a professional check it out, and have the seller fix it.

QUESTIONS TO ASK SELLER-AGENT?

When Was the Last Time the Air Conditioner Was Serviced? Why? What Was Done? ☐ yes ☐ no

If it has been a long time since the last servicing, the unit may soon need work. If it was recently serviced, find out what the problem was and how it was remedied. Ask to see estimates and invoices. Call the air-conditioning company—they can often give you a better explanation of the bill.

How Long Does It Take to Cool the Home? ☐ yes ☐ no

The seller may tell you it gets cool quickly, within an hour or so. Or, you may learn that the unit isn't big enough to actually cool down the house. Rather, the unit can only keep the house cool if it is started in the morning and left on all day. You want a unit that is big enough to cool down the house so it can then be turned off. Often, how well the air-conditioning works is more a function of the home's insulation than the efficiency of the unit. You may want to consider putting in new insulation and a new air conditioner when you move in.

Water Heater

QUESTIONS TO ASK YOURSELF

How Big Is the Heater?   ☐ yes   ☐ no

Today the minimum size is usually 50 gallons, although 40 gallons can be considered adequate if only one or two people are living in the home. A water heater that holds less than that won't provide enough hot water. And it will have to work too hard, adding to fuel costs.

What Type Is It?   ☐ yes   ☐ no

Typically water heaters are either gas or electric. Some heating systems, such as Amana, incorporate the water heater with the furnace to save on fuel costs. In the past, gas has been less expensive to operate because of low prices. However, with increased natural gas costs, electric water heaters may become competitive.

How Old Is It?   ☐ yes   ☐ no

The life span of a water heater (typically 7 to 20 years) depends a great deal on the quality and content of the water. Water with lots of sediment will soon fill up the bottom of the tank, reduce efficiency as well as volume, and require replacement sooner. Areas with strong electrostatic conditions or corrosives in the water will cause leaks more rapidly. A water heater costs between $200 and $500, depending on size and efficiency. Figure another $200 to have it installed. Newer heaters are far more efficient and use less fuel than older ones.

Is the Water Heater Tied Down? ☐ yes ☐ no

This is of special concern in earthquake and hurricane country. The heater should be permanently and securely attached to the walls so that it won't tip over under stress. Tipping can cause water, gas, and electric lines to rupture, causing fire and other damage. Ties cost under $50; installation would be about another $50.

Is the Water Heater Leaking? ☐ yes ☐ no

Look at the bottom of the water heater and under it (if possible). Check for leaks with your hand. (Be careful not to burn yourself on any hot areas!) A leaking water heater cannot be repaired—it must be replaced. Have the seller do it, but specify a bigger size or more efficient unit (and pay extra, if necessary).

Does It Have a Pressure Safety Valve? ☐ yes ☐ no

A pressure safety valve does not come with the heater, but *must* be added. It sits on top or on the side of the heater and has a small lever that can be lifted to test it. (In older units, sometimes lifting the levers causes the valve to malfunction and not shut off, requiring valve replacement.) This valve allows water and/or steam to safely escape should the heater controls seize up and not automatically turn off. It should be vented to the outside, to prevent burns. The cost is about $25 plus another $50 to $100 for installation. Have the seller pay for it.

Is There a Clean-Out?   ☐ yes   ☐ no

The water heater should have a drain. You can open it a little to see if water dribbles out. If it doesn't, the drain is plugged, and chances are, so is the heater. If the water that dribbles out has grains of sand or other sediment in it, this suggests that the heater is plugged.

Is the Vent in Place?   ☐ yes   ☐ no

A gas water heater will have a vent leading to the outside. This vent should be in place. If it is broken, badly dented, or off to one side, toxic gases may be released into the space the water heater occupies and, eventually, into the house. Don't try to fix it yourself, as it may be very hot. Have a professional deal with it and have the seller pay for repairs.

QUESTIONS TO ASK SELLER-AGENT

When Was the Heater Last Replaced?   ☐ yes   ☐ no

The seller will know if he or she replaced it. (There should also be a metal plate on the heater giving the date of manufacture.) If it's old, figure on having to replace it soon.

Are There Any Leaks?   ☐ yes   ☐ no

There may be leaks you didn't see. If so, insist that the seller replace the heater. Remember, it *cannot* be fixed.

Is the Capacity Sufficient? ☐ yes   ☐ no

Does the seller admit to running out of hot water? If so, the unit is insufficient. Remember, even a large heater may not produce much hot water if it is filled with sediment.

Water

QUESTIONS TO ASK YOURSELF

Is There Municipal Water or Is There a Well? ☐ yes   ☐ no

If there's a public water system, there should be a shutoff in front of the house leading out into the street. If there's a well, it will be identifiable somewhere on the property. Wells involve much more expense and maintenance.

Is the Water Soft or Hard? ☐ yes   ☐ no

Run the water and put a little soap on your hands. If it foams up quickly, chances are the water is soft. If few bubbles or foam form, chances are it's hard. Water softening systems can be installed, but usually there is a monthly maintenance fee, plus installation.

Does the Water Have a Bad Taste or Smell?

☐ yes   ☐ no

If it does, ask the seller-agent if the water throughout the area has these problems, or is it just in this house. Charcoal filters can be added to sink faucets to help remove bad taste and smell problems. The cost is typically around $100. If the problem is just with this one house, it should be thoroughly investigated by a plumber and a home inspector because it could be related to a health hazard. If it's areawide, check with the building and safety and local water department for an explanation.

Does the Water Have an Odd Color?

☐ yes   ☐ no

Potable water is normally colorless. If it has a blue color, there is copper leaching into the line. Other colors may indicate sediment, fecal material, or other contaminants. Take a sample of the water and have it analyzed.

QUESTIONS TO ASK SELLER-AGENT

Are There Any Water Problems?

☐ yes   ☐ no

If the answer is no, get it in writing. If yes, thoroughly investigate the problem. Some water problems cannot be solved, and you may want to pass on the house and even the area.

When Was the Well Last Tested?

☐ **yes**   ☐ **no**

All wells should be tested at least annually for contaminants. The testing can cost $100 or more. Ask to see the latest results. They should indicate two areas: bacterial levels and toxic contaminants. The report should indicate whether the water is pure enough for drinking. If it isn't, there may be no way to drill a new well and you may want to pass on the property.

Have There Been Any Well Problems?

☐ **yes**   ☐ **no**

Wells are subject to all sorts of problems. The pumps can break, the casing can collapse, or they can become contaminated. Be sure to have a well inspection by a professional.

5
Safety Issues

Detectors

QUESTIONS TO ASK YOURSELF

Is There a Smoke Detector?
☐ yes ☐ no

This is the number one safety device that will alert you if there is a fire in the home. Every building department in the country requires that they be installed in every home. If none are present, plan on installing them before you move in. They only cost around $10 and up.

Is There a Smoke Detector in Every Bedroom, on Every Floor, and in All Living Areas?
☐ yes ☐ no

Most building departments require smoke detectors in all of these areas. That means that a typical three-bedroom house could have as many as five to seven detectors to meet local building code. That's a small price to pay for fire safety.

Are All Smoke Detectors Operational?

☐ yes   ☐ no

Fire detectors are easy to test. They normally have a button on the front. Just depress the button until a loud screaming sound is heard. If no sound erupts, the battery is probably dead or the detector itself is damaged and should be replaced.

Is the Detector Battery-Powered or Hardwired?

☐ yes   ☐ no

Batteries can go dead, but the home electrical system is often the first thing knocked out in a fire. Many building departments insist on both kinds of smoke detectors. You can determine what kind you have by gently removing the cover from the wall (usually by turning the covering plate). A battery-operated smoke detector will have a battery in it. A home system will have wiring leading into the wall. Some sophisticated units will have both.

Are Units Ion-Chamber or Photoelectric?

☐ yes   ☐ no

Ion-chamber is good for detecting hot fires and is the cheapest to buy. Photoelectric is good for smoky fires, but costs $25 and up. Both should be used; sometimes both are incorporated in the same unit. Look on the label.

Are the Smoke Detectors in an Unobstructed Location?

☐ yes   ☐ no

Detectors can only work if fire and smoke can get to them. If they are placed in corners or closets, they may never get their warning out in time. Plan to move poorly located units to better areas. Keep in mind, however, that if you remove a unit from a ceiling or a wall, it may leave a bare or dirty spot that needs repainting or replastering.

Is There a Carbon Monoxide Detector?

☐ **yes**   ☐ **no**

Every house should have at least one. Carbon monoxide is odorless and colorless and kills by preventing the body from absorbing oxygen. Carbon monoxide comes from gas- or oil-burning furnaces, heaters, or stoves that are badly vented. If no detector is present, plan on buying one. They cost around $50.

QUESTIONS TO ASK SELLER-AGENT

Where Are the Smoke Detectors?

☐ **yes**   ☐ **no**

They may not be self-evident, but they could be there. The seller will know where they are, if any are present, and can point them out to you. Test each one, as indicated above.

Have There Been Any Previous Fires in the Home?

☐ **yes**   ☐ **no**

This is a good time to ask. The home may look perfectly okay, but there could have been severe fire damage that was cosmetically covered up. The seller should disclose any previous fire damage. Have a thorough professional inspection to determine that repairs were properly made.

Asbestos

QUESTIONS TO ASK YOURSELF

What Is the Danger from Asbestos in the Home?

☐ yes ☐ no

The American Lung Association has linked asbestos fibers to increased risk of asbestosis (lung scarring), mesothelioma (cancer of the abdominal cavity), and lung cancer. Although high concentrations are usually necessary to produce a problem, it is not known what problems a minimal amount of asbestos can cause. The safest course is to have no asbestos in the home.

Are There "Popcorn" Ceilings?

☐ yes ☐ no

Popular in the 1950s and 1960s, these ceilings (also sometimes called "acoustical") have a plaster sprayed on that looks a little bit like popcorn. The plaster often contained asbestos. If not disturbed, there is often no problem. Sealing with a coating of shellac or similar product and then painting will help to encapsulate the asbestos-plaster and prevent it from entering the air.

Are There Vinyl Floors?

☐ yes ☐ no

Vinyl-asbestos flooring has been very popular. It's usually found in squares, but can be in whole floor products. Again, if not disturbed, it may not be a problem. It should only be removed by a professional asbestos mitigation company. The cost can be thousands of dollars per room, as special breathing equipment is required and the material is treated as a toxic waste.

What About Wrappings on Pipes and Ducts?

☐ yes   ☐ no

These may be visible in the home, garage, or attic. If properly wrapped and sealed, there should be no problem. If torn open, however, asbestos fibers may be released into the air. No attempt should be made to fix this by anyone other than a professional asbestos mitigation company. Again, expect the cost to be anywhere from a few hundred to many thousands of dollars. If there's an existing problem, be sure the seller takes care of it.

Is There Any Asbestos Elsewhere?

☐ yes   ☐ no

Asbestos can be found in older roof insulation, artificial embers for fireplaces, and door gaskets on furnaces. It often looks white and flaky; however, positive identification can only be made using a microscope. If you suspect asbestos, get a professional inspector to check for it. The cost is often around $100 for lab work.

QUESTIONS TO ASK SELLER-AGENT

When Was the Home Built?

☐ yes   ☐ no

Homes built after 1978 generally do not have asbestos in the plaster, although it may still be used as insulation for ductwork and pipes and elsewhere.

Has Any Part of the House Ever Been Tested for Asbestos? ☐ yes ☐ no

The test will be on record and the seller should tell you about it and let you see the results. If the seller says no, get it in writing, to protect yourself should you later discover that it was, in fact, tested. Find out what part of the home was tested.

If Asbestos Was Found, How Was It Ameliorated? ☐ yes ☐ no

Removal or encapsulation of asbestos is usually acceptable. Be sure a professional asbestos mitigation company, not the seller, did the work. Ask to see the final report from the company. If the seller did the work, demand an inspection.

Are There Any Known Asbestos Problems in Other Homes in the Neighborhood? ☐ yes ☐ no

Often with homes built in a tract, where one home has asbestos in a particular location, all will have it. In fact, there may be a well-known asbestos problem. The agent can most likely provide you with more information.

Lead

QUESTIONS TO ASK YOURSELF

What Is Lead Poisoning?

☐ yes ☐ no

Lead poisoning can cause a wide variety of symptoms, from high blood pressure to retardation. Death can result from long exposure to lead. It affects children more than adults. In the home, lead usually comes from old lead-based paint.

How Old Is the Home?

☐ yes ☐ no

The major contamination from lead in the home comes from lead-based paints, which were outlawed in 1978. However, homes built a year or two later might still have some lead-based paints as builders used up existing supplies. The owner should be able to tell you the age; then you should confirm it with the building department. An old trick is to turn over the cover of the toilet bowl tank. The date of manufacture is usually stamped there and unless the tank was replaced, it should be about the date when the home was built.

Is the Paint Oil Based?

☐ yes ☐ no

Although lead can be in both latex and oil paints, it is mostly associated with oil paints because they have been around longer. Oil paints often have a much higher gloss. Look for this, particularly in older homes.

Is There Any Paint Flaking or "Dusting" Inside or Out?
☐ yes   ☐ no

Although lead is stable in paint (unless it is chewed by little children), as the paint ages it can dry out and dust off. The dust contains lead and can contaminate the ground outside as well as parts of the home inside. Any flaking or "dusting" paint should be regarded as suspicious.

How Old Is the Copper Piping?
☐ yes   ☐ no

Until just a few years ago, lead-based solder was used to connect copper piping. Studies have shown that this solder can leach into the water and result in a lead hazard. However, after about five years of usage, the leaching effect generally stops.

Should You Buy a Home That Is Contaminated with Lead?
☐ yes   ☐ no

The seller must present you with a statement regarding lead in the home. However, the language in the statement is vague. You have 10 days after receiving this statement to rescind the deal without penalty, according to federal law. Keep in mind, however, that some people have lived safely with lead paint for years. The biggest concern is if you have small children who might chew on windowsills, doors, and so forth and thus poison themselves. For more information, check with the National Lead Information Center (800-424-LEAD—www.epa.govlead/nlic.htm).

QUESTIONS TO ASK THE SELLER-AGENT

Has the Home Ever Been Tested for Lead?
☐ yes ☐ no

The testing costs between $300 and $500. Very few homes have been tested. If the owner says this home was tested, and unless you are told differently, you should assume that lead was found. Ask to see the report. If not available, get the name of the company and call or write for a copy of the report.

If Tested, Where Was the Lead Found?
☐ yes ☐ no

Ask the seller to show you the area. Is it a large area requiring that a lot of paint be removed? Or is it a small area encompassing just a few boards?

How Was It Eliminated?
☐ yes ☐ no

Unlike asbestos, lead cannot be safely encapsulated. It must be professionally removed. Lead paint cannot be safely scraped, burned, or sanded off. Sometimes the only remedy is to remove whatever the lead was painted on. Lead paint removal for an entire house can easily cost $10,000 to $15,000 and up. If lead paint is a serious problem, demand that the seller pay to have it removed, or look for another house. (If you buy a house with lead-paint problems, remember, you'll have the same trouble when it's time to resell.)

Formaldehyde

QUESTIONS TO ASK YOURSELF

Are There Any Strong, Acrid Odors in the Home?

☐ yes ☐ no

Formaldehyde is easy to recognize. It's the odor that came from the preservative used to pickle frogs in high school biology classes. The pungent, colorless gas can cause allergy attacks, eye and throat irritation, and has been linked to cancer by the Environmental Protection Agency (EPA). You're more likely to detect formaldehyde if all the windows in the home were closed for a few days.

Is There Any Veneer Paneling?

☐ yes ☐ no

Older paneling was made with formaldehyde, and it often gave off the odor. However, over time the smell gradually diminishes. Sniff around wall paneling. Also, check near other walls, since it has been used in insulation, particularly in mobile homes.

Are Any Cabinets Giving Off Odors?

☐ yes ☐ no

Some cabinetry, particularly made of some types of pressed woods, contains formaldehyde. Open the cabinets and sniff around.

QUESTIONS TO ASK THE SELLER-AGENT

Is There Any Formaldehyde in the Home?

☐ yes   ☐ no

If there is and the seller knows about it, he or she will usually admit it. Ask if it has presented any problems. Ask if this is the reason they are selling the home!

If So, How Was It Treated?

☐ yes   ☐ no

Usually the only way to treat formaldehyde is to either remove the products producing the odor, or install a good ventilation system. Product removal is best. Check to see what was done.

Radon

QUESTIONS TO ASK SELLER-AGENT

Has the Home Ever Been Checked for Radon Gas?

☐ yes   ☐ no

Radon is a radioactive gas that is odorless and colorless and usually is drawn into homes, particularly the basements and lower floors, from the earth. It is not found in all geographic areas. The only way to check for it is to set up a radon detection unit, which samples the air, and then have it sent off for analysis. The minimal amount of time for sampling is typically one month.

Have Any Homes in the Area Had Radon Gas?

☐ yes   ☐ no

If there is radon known to be in other nearby homes, chances are it's in this one as well. Radon is the second leading cause of lung cancer in the United States, according to the Surgeon General. However, there is usually a very long period of exposure required before illness occurs.

Is This an Area Where Radon Gas Is Common?

☐ yes   ☐ no

Some geological areas are more likely to have radon gas than others are. In areas in which radon is common, the building department will often have prepared white papers on the subject. Check with them.

How Was the Home Treated for Radon Gas?

☐ yes   ☐ no

A radon reduction system usually consists of a clean-air ventilator installed in the lower levels of a home. The price can be anywhere from $1000 to $5000. If the home has been identified as having radon, be sure the seller either corrects the problem or gives you an allowance against the purchase price for its correction.

6
Land and Landscaping

View

QUESTIONS TO ASK YOURSELF

Does the Property Have a View? ☐ yes ☐ no

A lot with a view is always more desirable. Depending on what the view is, it can increase the value of the property quite a bit, sometimes twice what the home and lot are worth.

Does the Lot Face the View? ☐ yes ☐ no

A view is only good as long as you can see it. A view in the front or side of a property is not nearly as good as one in the rear. The reason is that most people today sit in their backyard, not on their front porch.

Does the Home Face the View?

☐ yes   ☐ no

Some homes don't take advantage of a view. I've seen tract homes plopped on a view lot where the only way you could see the view was out the bathroom window. A lot with a view, but a with a house on it that doesn't take advantage of that view, is worth much less.

Is There Anything Obstructing the View?

☐ yes   ☐ no

Some views are partial. You could have a view of a lake or the ocean, but only over the top of a building next to yours. An obstructed view is worth less than an unobstructed one. A view of the mountains from a tiny corner of the backyard probably adds nothing to the value of the home.

Is There Anything That Could Obstruct the View in the Future?

☐ yes   ☐ no

The marvelous view the home has today could be completely obscured if a tall building is put up next door, or by trees growing tall over time. In most cases there is no "right to a view." That means that if your neighbor obscures your view, you may find you cannot force your neighbor to restore it.

How Much Extra Am I Paying for the View?

☐ yes   ☐ no

Find out how much a similar house without a view is selling for. Subtract the difference; that's the cost of your view. Ask yourself if it's worth it to you. Ask yourself what will the house be worth if something happens to the view?

QUESTIONS TO ASK THE SELLER-AGENT

Are There Any Lawsuits over the View?

☐ yes   ☐ no

Some of the bitterest lawsuits result when a neighbor obscures a view, often because of the growth of trees. I've seen individuals and home-owner associations (HOAs) spend hundreds of thousands of dollars on lawsuits in these types of cases. If there have been lawsuits in the past, be wary of neighbors who are sensitized and who may be prepared to go to court again because of a similar issue.

Have There Been Any Arguments with Neighbors over the View?

☐ yes   ☐ no

It's best to have friendly relations with your neighbors. This may be impossible if there is already an argument in progress. You may decide you don't want to buy into an existing altercation.

Are There Any Building Development Plans That Could Affect the View?

☐ yes   ☐ no

New homes, a commercial development, a large art piece, almost any-thing can be in the works months or even years down the road. If the seller-agent isn't sure, check with the local planning commission.

Boundaries

QUESTIONS TO ASK YOURSELF

What Are the Property's Boundaries?

☐ **yes** ☐ **no**

Sometimes a lot will extend far beyond what appears to be a peripheral fence. If so, it can mean much more maintenance for you than you anticipated. Other times, the fence will be in a neighbor's yard, meaning your yard is actually smaller than you thought. It's a good idea to insist on a survey to determine the true boundaries of the property you're buying.

Do You Have Adequate Ingress and Egress?

☐ **yes** ☐ **no**

This is not usually a problem; however, sometimes a lot doesn't extend all the way to the street. To get in and out you must travel over someone else's lot. If those people decide to put a fence across your ingress-egress, you could have a landlocked lot, which can reduce its value to a fraction of what you paid.

Are There Any Utility Poles on or Near the Property?

☐ **yes** ☐ **no**

Sometimes utility companies have easements across lots. High-voltage utility poles, besides looking unattractive, have created concerns about health issues. Even if studies suggest no health problems, that concern can reduce property values and make it much more difficult to resell the property later on.

Are There Any "Rights-of-Way" across the Property? ☐ yes ☐ no

People walking across a lot can make a trail that, over time, can become a right-of-way that you may not be able to close. Other homeowners may have the right to travel across your property. Investigate any trails, paths, or roads leading across the lot.

QUESTIONS TO ASK SELLER-AGENT

Are There Any Easements? ☐ yes ☐ no

These could be rights-of-way, utility companies' rights, or other rights granted to others affecting the lot. They may be harmless, or they could reduce the lot's value. Also, check the title company's preliminary report.

Are There Any Encroachments? ☐ yes ☐ no

Is part of a neighbor's house on your lot? If so, it could make it difficult to finance your purchase or to resell. Make sure the seller removes the encroachment before you buy.

Soils and Rocks

QUESTIONS TO ASK YOURSELF

Is the Soil Suitable for Planting?

□ yes　　□ no

If your heart's desire is a rock garden, substandard soil will be of no consequence to you. On the other hand, if you plan on a lush growing garden, the soil can help or hinder. If the soil is very bad, you'll have to bring in suitable topsoil. Plan on $500 for a medium-size backyard. A soil's report will tell you the condition of the soil, or check with a good gardener.

Is the Soil Rocky?

□ yes　　□ no

Rocks are the enemy of gardeners. Rocky soil means you'll spend time, effort, and/or money preparing the ground. Some soils have huge boulders that actually have to be removed by dynamiting! If the yard has very rocky soil and you're looking forward to gardening, it might be better to choose a different property.

Is the Soil Friable?

□ yes　　□ no

Good soil isn't compacted. It allows water to flow easily through it, which is great for planting. Sometimes oil appears rich, but actually isn't friable. Again, ask a good gardener or get a soils report.

Is the Soil Made of Clay and Is It Expansive?

☐ yes ☐ no

Clay soil tends to expand when wet. As a consequence, it can break foundations and cause deep cracks in slabs. If the soil is clay, be sure to have a thorough inspection of the foundation and slab (if any). Footings should be at least 18 inches deep and 12 inches wide in clay soil (much deeper in freezing climates)—ask a professional inspector to check this out, or check with the local building department about the original plans for the home.

Is the Soil Gravelly?

☐ yes ☐ no

Gravelly soil is usually the best for holding a foundation. It also makes the soil friable, as long as the soil is made up of about even amounts of gravel and dirt.

Does the Soil Have Organics?

☐ yes ☐ no

Avoid homes that are built on peat bogs. The soil may look normal, but if it has too much organic material on it, it will always be wet, it can sink, and it can even catch fire in a very dry season!

QUESTIONS TO ASK THE SELLER-AGENT

Have You Had a Soils Inspection?

☐ yes ☐ no

Don't expect a yes answer here. However, if there has been an inspection, suspect a problem and be sure to get a copy of the report.

Have You Had Any Soil Problems of Any Kind?   ☐ yes   ☐ no

Make this as broad a query as possible. Soil problems can ruin a house. If any are revealed, insist on a soils report and have a competent engineering specialist analyze it.

Does Water Pool or Absorb into the Ground?   ☐ yes   ☐ no

This simple observation by the seller can help you quickly determine what kind of soil the property has. This is particularly useful if you're buying in the summer and don't otherwise have a clue what the soil will be like in winter.

Utilities

QUESTIONS TO ASK YOURSELF

Is There Electricity at the Property?   ☐ yes   ☐ no

This is something we all expect. However, in some rural areas electricity has not yet been brought to the property, so a home system (for example, a generator, windmill, or solar setup) must be used, or, alternatively, a local municipal system. Lack of a utility is a serious drawback. Connecting later can cost a great deal of money.

Is There Potable Water? Is There a Well?

☐ yes   ☐ no

Again, most urban areas have a well-developed potable water distribution system. Many rural areas, however, use community wells or an individual well on each property. With municipal water systems, there is usually only the cost of the water itself. With wells, there are often other costs for maintenance and replacement. A well system can be twice as expensive to run, proportionately, as a municipal water system.

Is There a Cable TV System?

☐ yes   ☐ no

Though certainly not as important these days with satellite direct systems, cable access is considered a necessity by some. Over-the-air reception is largely passé in most areas because of the relatively few channels available.

Is There Adequate Phone Service?

☐ yes   ☐ no

If you have an electrical utility connection, chances are you also have phone service, since they often share the same delivery system. A big question for many is the bandwidth. Are fiber-optic, high-speed cable lines or digital subscriber line (DSL) services available in the area for fast Internet access?

Is Natural Gas Connected?

□ yes   □ no

Natural gas is piped to over 40 million homes in the United States. However, that leaves many homes without natural gas. In some cases, particularly in rural areas, propane tanks are delivered to the property. In other cases, the homes are all-electric. Not having natural gas can affect the type of appliances you have as well as the cost of heating and running your home. Until recently, natural gas was significantly less expensive than other forms of energy.

QUESTIONS TO ASK THE SELLER-AGENT

Are There Any Utility Bonds?

□ yes   □ no

Bringing utilities to your property costs money. If the utility company is privately owned, it often absorbs these costs. However, in cases where a municipal utility is involved, bonds are floated to pay for these costs. Are any of these bonds still on the property? Will the seller pay them off prior to close of escrow?

Are There Frequent Service Disruptions?

□ yes   □ no

Frequent local service disruptions indicate a badly run utility. Besides the inconvenience, this can come back to haunt you in the form of higher bills as the utility strives to improve its equipment.

Are There Any Utility Easements? Where?

☐ yes ☐ no

An easement is the right of the utility to use part of your property for its own purposes, such as putting in a new line. Usually you cannot build or develop land over a utility easement. Find out where any easements are. Have the seller point them out, or if the seller doesn't know, check the plot plan that should be provided to you by the title insurance company used to insure your purchase. Make sure you can live with the easements, because you cannot get rid of them later.

Are There Any Special Increased Delivery Fees?

☐ yes ☐ no

Sometimes there are special assessments to pay for the installation of utility poles or water mains. These assessments can double your normal utility bills, and the payments must be made for many years.

When Was the Well Water Last Tested? What Were the Results?

☐ yes ☐ no

If the property has a well, the water should be tested for bacteria, minerals, and chemicals at least once a year. Ask to see the last test results. Are there any problems with the water? If so, you might need to rebuild the existing well or put in a new one. The cost at minimum is likely to be $5000.

Have There Been Any Problems with the Well?

☐ yes ☐ no

While the well water may be pure, the well itself may not function well. It may need new casings or a pump motor. Get the well inspected by a specialist. A new well pump can easily cost $500 to $1500, depending on the depth and capacity you need.

Driveways and Walkways

DRIVEWAYS—QUESTIONS TO ASK YOURSELF

Is There an Adequate Driveway?

☐ **yes**   ☐ **no**

The driveway should be wide enough to accommodate the size of the garage. Normally, a two-car garage will have a driveway wide enough for two cars. If it's a very long driveway, or the garage has more than two bays, a narrow driveway is fine, provided there is an adequate turn-around space in front of the garage. If the driveway is too short or too narrow, be wary. It can cost many thousands of dollars to expand it. A brand-new, short, two-lane driveway can easily cost between $2500 and $5000, or more.

What Is the Driveway Made Of?

☐ **yes**   ☐ **no**

The most commonly used materials (cement, brick, asphalt, and gravel) each have pros and cons. Brick tends to be the hardiest and tends to look the best; however, it can crack or buckle, and grass growing between the bricks can be a constant maintenance problem. Cement is likewise hardy and looks good, but cracks can require very costly repairs. Asphalt is less expensive and is subject to cracking at the edges, especially in freezing weather, but can be inexpensively repaired. Gravel is the least expensive, doesn't look as good, and tends to get "lost" amidst dirt and weeds.

If Cement, Are There Significant Cracks?

☐ yes ☐ no

Most cement has hairline cracks that can be ignored. Cracks larger than ⅛ inch, however, suggest ground movement underneath (or tree roots), especially if one edge is displaced higher or lower than the other. This problem can be more severe if reinforcement bars or wire mesh was not used when the driveway was poured. Cracks quickly make a cement driveway look old and worn, detracting from the overall appearance of the house. Sometimes, depending on location, cracks can be cut out of a cement driveway and replaced by a row of bricks or new cement. This is far less costly than replacing the entire driveway.

If Cement, Does It Have Red Rust Stains?

☐ yes ☐ no

Rust stains usually occur when a car parked on the driveway leaks from its radiator. These stains can also occur from any iron object that is left to rust on the driveway. Rust stains are very unsightly and hard to remove, although chemicals are sold commercially that claim to do so. I've found they are not all that effective. You may want to demand that the seller clean the driveway before completing the purchase.

If Cement, Does It Have Tar and Oil Stains?

☐ yes ☐ no

Again, these stains usually come from a car that was parked on the driveway. Most tar and oil stains can be removed using a variety of commercially sold chemicals. A clean driveway adds to the appearance, and value, of a home. A stained driveway detracts.

If Asphalt, Are There Significant Bulges?

☐ yes   ☐ no

Asphalt is soft and somewhat pliable, especially in a hot summer. Tree roots can cause it to bulge in an unsightly way. The only remedy is to dig through the asphalt and remove the root, then repave that area. The cost can be a few hundred dollars for a small section, or significantly more for a larger portion of the driveway.

If Asphalt, Are There Alligator Cracks?

☐ yes   ☐ no

Most asphalt driveways do not have an adequate shoulder to protect them. As a result, the edges tend to break off, causing cracks that look like an alligator's skin. At an early stage, this process can be greatly slowed by applying tar and a cover coating. If left unchecked, this deterioration will cause large chunks of the asphalt to break away, requiring a total repaving of the driveway.

If Gravel, Are There Grasses and Weeds Growing Through?

☐ yes   ☐ no

Gravel driveways require constant maintenance. They must be weeded (or a weed killer sprayed on), and leaves and dirt must be removed. If a gravel driveway is not maintained, it can disappear into the ground in five years, requiring that a new driveway be put in.

Is the Driveway Circular?

☐ yes   ☐ no

Circular driveways, where you drive in an entrance and out a separate exit, are considered more desirable than one-entrance driveways (where you must back out). Circular driveways usually add value to a property.

WALKWAYS—QUESTIONS TO ASK YOURSELF

Is There a Sidewalk in Front of the House?

☐ yes   ☐ no

Most tract homes have front sidewalks. Some custom homes and houses in rural areas do not. Generally speaking, a sidewalk is a plus. However, in a custom area a lack of a sidewalk may contribute to an overall "country" look, which many consider desirable. A tract area that does not have a sidewalk, however, may simply indicate a poorly designed development.

Is the Sidewalk Cracked or Bulged?

☐ yes   ☐ no

You may be happy to buy a home with a broken sidewalk. But if someone trips and falls on it, you could be financially liable. Sometimes a city will fix your sidewalk and then send you the bill, which can be quite steep. Replacement of only a few feet of sidewalk can easily cost $250 to $1000.

Is There a Separate Walkway to the House?

☐ yes   ☐ no

Some builders save money by linking the front door of the house to the driveway. A more desirable appearance is achieved when there is a separate walkway from the front door to the sidewalk and/or street.

Is the Walkway Cement or Is It Stepping Stones?

☐ yes   ☐ no

A cement walkway will last longer and be easier to maintain, as long as it doesn't crack. Stepping stones are generally considered to be a temporary walkway, although if done well, they can add an artistic flair to the home's appearance.

QUESTIONS TO ASK THE SELLER-AGENT

Have You Had Any Problems with the Driveway or Walkway? ☐ yes ☐ no

If there has been a recent repair, it might be disguising a recurring problem with cracking, buckling, bulging, or whatever. This could be a costly problem for you in the future.

Have You Replaced the Driveway or the Walkway? ☐ yes ☐ no

If the seller has replaced the driveway or walkway, you should ask why? Was the problem solved? Is it likely to recur?

Landscaping

QUESTIONS TO ASK YOURSELF

Is the Front Yard Attractively Landscaped? ☐ yes ☐ no

A well-landscaped front yard makes the house look more valuable. Beware of buying the landscaping and not the house. On the other hand, a badly landscaped front yard detracts from value, and could get you a bargain price. Hiring a gardener to redo a landscape can cost from $2000 to $10,000. Or you could do it yourself for the cost of the plants and lawn materials.

Is the Backyard Attractively Landscaped?

☐ yes   ☐ no

A good-looking backyard makes the house more livable, but usually doesn't add much to its market price. Don't be fooled into paying more for an attractive backyard. Most buyers of homes with poorly land-scaped backyards fix them up slowly and inexpensively over time.

Is There a Sprinkler or Drip System?

☐ yes   ☐ no

The installation of a complete system can cost several thousand dollars.

Does It Cover All the Bushes, Shrubs, and Trees As Well As the Lawn?

☐ yes   ☐ no

Many systems simply cover the lawn, meaning you'll need to hand water everything else. If you're looking for a low-maintenance yard, you'll want one with complete sprinkler and/or drip system coverage.

Is There a Preponderance of Cement or Live Ground Cover in the Back and Side Yards?

☐ yes   ☐ no

More cement means less maintenance. More ground cover means more work taking care of it. However, the cement must be attractively done, or else it will detract from, instead of add to, the appearance of the yard.

Is There a Fountain?

☐ yes   ☐ no

Some people find a bubbling fountain attractive. Is it working? Fountains tend to break and can cost upward of $100 or more to repair each time. How old is it? The older the fountain, the more likely it is to become a problem. Hiring someone to remove and dispose of an old fountain can cost several hundred dollars.

Is There Accent Lighting?

☐ yes   ☐ no

"Malibu" or other types of lighting can make a yard very attractive. However, fancy lighting should not figure into your valuation of a property. A wired low-voltage system or a wireless solar-powered system only costs around $100 or less, and you can put one in yourself in an afternoon.

Are There Overhead Lights?

☐ yes   ☐ no

Lights mounted on poles are usually wired into the home's 110-V system. If the lights are located some distance from the house, they can be quite costly to have installed, upward of $500 to $1000 or more, depending on distance and number. If the lights are needed for a long driveway or walkway and there are none, consider installing them to eventually enhance the resale value of the property.

QUESTIONS TO ASK THE SELLER-AGENT

Was the Landscaping Professionally Done?

☐ yes   ☐ no

Usually you can tell just by looking. However, beautifully done landscaping is a valuable asset to a home, whether done by a professional or a talented homeowner.

Were Permits Obtained As Needed for Work Done?

☐ yes   ☐ no

Many municipalities require permits for all sorts of work, including the installation of sprinklers and/or a drip system, cement pads, decks, lighting, and so forth. If done without permit (as they often are), they may be incorrectly installed and, in the case of electrical and plumbing work, could present a health hazard and a financial liability to you. Ask the seller to bring all substandard work up to code.

Was There Additional Work Planned, but Not Completed?

☐ yes   ☐ no

Sometimes the organization of a yard simply doesn't make sense. Ask the seller about it. It might turn out that it's only 70 percent completed. When the plan for the remaining 30 percent is explained, the yard's landscaping will become clearer. Ask the seller to finish the work, or give you an allowance so that it can be completed.

Bushes and Shrubs

QUESTIONS TO ASK YOURSELF

Are Bushes Placed around the Property?

☐ yes   ☐ no

Bushes provide accent and privacy. They are best placed at the edges of property and along fences and walls. Bushes in the center of a yard often draw too much attention to themselves and may need to be removed or replanted elsewhere, at your expense after you buy the home.

Do the Bushes Complement the Landscaping?   ☐ yes   ☐ no

Different varieties of bushes grow at different rates and to different heights and widths. A bush that grows to 7 feet high that is placed in an area where a shorter look is desired requires constant trimming. Bushes in front of the home that are too tall or too wide will hide the home. Bushes that were planted to increase privacy but are too short for their location will not serve that purpose. Do the bushes complement the overall landscaping, or will you need to replace them after the purchase? Hiring a gardener to plant a simple row of bushes can cost $400 or more, depending on the plants used and the distance covered.

QUESTIONS TO ASK THE SELLER-AGENT

Are All Bushes in Compliance with the Homeowner's Association's Rules or their Covenants, Conditions, and Restrictions (CC&Rs)?   ☐ yes   ☐ no

In some developments, the size, type, and placement of bushes are closely regulated, especially in front yards. For example, bushes might not be allowed to be more than 3 feet tall along the front edge of a property. Ask the seller if the bushes are in compliance with the rules. Ask to see the rules to be sure.

Are the Bushes Evergreen, or Will They Lose Their Leaves in Winter?   ☐ yes   ☐ no

Some bushes are evergreen the year round. Others drop their leaves and develop berries in the winter. Others simply hibernate in the winter and appear dead until spring (roses are an example). This can dramatically alter the appearance of the yard for the worse during the winter months. If you're not sure, ask the seller.

Are Any Bushes Unhealthy?

☐ yes   ☐ no

If any of the bushes appear unhealthy, ask the seller if there are any growing problems. Some soils contain chemicals of one sort or another that hinder growth. Cleansing the soil or providing special nutrients can cost hundreds of dollars.

Lawn

QUESTIONS TO ASK YOURSELF

Is There a Front Lawn?

☐ yes   ☐ no

A front lawn is not mandatory, but for almost all homes, it creates a welcoming appearance that is important to most people. In the southwest, rock gardens and cacti may replace lawns because of water shortages. A house without a front lawn or without some sort of landscaping will show poorly, and will usually command a lower price. It costs about $1500 to $2000 to put in an average new front lawn from sod.

Is There a Lawn in the Backyard?

☐ yes   ☐ no

Lawns are less frequently found in backyards, and many people consider landscaping in the backyard to be an expensive idea. A backyard lawn requires constant mowing and upkeep. On the other hand, trees, shrubs, paths, pools, spas, decks, and other desirable features can lead to a low-maintenance backyard.

Do the Lawns Have Sprinklers?

☐ **yes**　　☐ **no**

Every lawn should have a sprinkler system, or it will not be watered properly. In parts of the Midwest and East where there is heavy rainfall year round, a sprinkler system may not be necessary. However, if a lawn is not watered in warm weather for even just a week, it can begin to die. It can cost upward of $2000 for a properly installed lawn sprinkler system, including permits.

Are the Sprinklers on an Automatic Timer?

☐ **yes**　　☐ **no**

There's no point in having a lawn sprinkler system if it's not on a timer. Only the most fastidious owner will remember to regularly turn the water on and off manually. It costs about $250, not counting labor, to convert to an automatic system.

Do the Lawns Look Green and Healthy?

☐ **yes**　　☐ **no**

You don't need an expert to tell you whether the lawn is in good shape. Brown spots, bare spots, thin spots, and mixed grasses all indicate a problem. It does, however, usually take a good gardener to come up with a solution and a cost for fixing a lawn that is in poor shape. Get an estimate.

Are There Weeds in the Lawns?

☐ **yes**　　☐ **no**

Some people require only that a lawn be full and green. Others demand that it all be the same type of grass. Know what *you* want. A lawn that's full of crabgrass and other weeds may need to be removed and replanted to get it perfect. The cost could easily be $2000 or more, even for a small lawn.

Is the Lawn Flat for Easy Mowing?

☐ **yes** ☐ **no**

A flat lawn is a real plus if you're planning on mowing it yourself. If it's sloped, plan on spending around $300 for a mower that has a powered wheel drive, or hire a gardener.

Do the Lawns Have Defined Edges for Easy Trimming?

☐ **yes** ☐ **no**

Grass will grow everywhere it has a chance. Cement, wood, or plastic borders help keep the lawn where it belongs. If there aren't any defined edges, you'll want to install them. They are inexpensive (under $50), but the work is hard.

Are There Any Depressions in the Lawns?

☐ **yes** ☐ **no**

Holes or depressions mean that water will pool either from rain runoff or sprinkler watering. Standing water will destroy the lawn and can cause odors and health problems (mosquitoes). Often a drain must be installed, at a cost of several hundred dollars or more, to remove standing water.

QUESTIONS TO ASK THE SELLER-AGENT

Do the Lawns Turn Yellow and/or Brown in Winter?

☐ **yes** ☐ **no**

Some grasses are annuals, meaning they die back in winter. There's nothing wrong with this, as long as it doesn't bother you. Modern grasses are often blends that remain green all year.

Do Puddles Form in the Lawn When Watering?

☐ **yes**   ☐ **no**

If so, you may want to insist that the seller install a drainage system, or give you an allowance for one, before completing the purchase.

Is There an Automatic Sprinkler System?

☐ **yes**   ☐ **no**

If not, consider the cost of putting one in when you make your offer on the home. Also, be sure to ask if the system adequately covers the entire lawn. A brown spot could be the result of an area that gets little to no water.

What's the Name and Phone Number of the Seller's Gardener?

☐ **yes**   ☐ **no**

If it's not broken, don't fix it. If you like the appearance of the lawn, why not hire the gardener who's been responsible for it?

Trees

QUESTIONS TO ASK YOURSELF

Does the Property Have Trees?

☐ **yes**   ☐ **no**

Healthy, mature trees are pleasant to look at and add significantly to a home's value. When it comes time to resell, the next buyers will look more favorably on a property with good trees. You may find that a treed property sells for as much as 5 to 10 percent more than a barren lot.

Are the Trees Matched to the Home? ☐ yes ☐ no

Trees should match the overall style of the home. Palm trees don't go with a New England cottage and liquid ambars don't fit a southwest Spanish décor. The trees should fit the style of the home. If they don't, you may need to cut them down and replace them—an expensive process. (It could cost $500 or more to fell a tall tree.)

Are the Trees Overly Tall or Crowded? ☐ yes ☐ no

A line of flowing cypress trees can be magnificent, but if they're 40 feet tall towering over a flat-roofed, single-story house, they will stand out like a sore thumb. On the other hand, trees in the front yard can add privacy. Too many, however, hide the home and can make it look like a mystery house from a horror movie. Sometimes with trees, less can be more.

Are There Fruit Trees? ☐ yes ☐ no

Fruit-bearing trees are a big plus—they produce oranges, apples, plums, or whatever. However, they can also leave a big mess that you'll be cleaning up every summer or fall. Fruit trees are generally better in the backyard than in the front.

Do the Trees Shade the House? ☐ yes ☐ no

Shade trees can reduce your cooling expenses in summer. Check to see that they are on the southern side of the house to offer the most shade. Trees placed on the northern side are unlikely to afford much protection from the sun.

Are There Any Deciduous Trees?

☐ yes   ☐ no

Maples and sycamores are lovely to look at and provide shade. But, in the fall you can spend whole weekends cleaning up around them, raking and disposing of leaves. Be sure it's something you don't mind doing before buying a home with lots of deciduous trees.

Are There Any Trees Near the Swimming Pool?

☐ yes   ☐ no

Trees and bushes drop their leaves when there's a wind, especially deciduous trees in the fall, as noted above. If the leaves fall into a swimming pool, they can not only clog filters but also provide the organic material that algae love. It's far harder to keep a pool clean when there are leaves falling into it on a regular basis. To keep your pool clean, you'll need to relandscape around it, removing trees and bushes.

Are There Any Young Trees That Will Grow Tall Near the Foundation, Driveway, or Walkways?

☐ yes   ☐ no

As trees grow, their root system spreads out to their drip line or beyond. Big trees mean big roots, which can crack foundations or driveways. Any trees that are within 10 feet of the foundation, driveway, or a walkway could be a problem. Be wary of trees such as pines, which look lovely when they are immature, but can grow to 100 feet tall with huge roots.

Are There any Big Trees Growing Over or Near the Sewer Line? ☐ yes ☐ no

Over time, their roots could break into the line, resulting in costly repairs. (It can cost $2500 and up to dig up and replace a sewer to the street.) To determine if trees are over the sewer line, locate the toilet closest to the front of the house and then imagine a line from it perpendicular to the street; the sewer line will probably be below. A more accurate diagram may be available from the original building plans filed with the city and/or county building and planning department when the home was constructed.

QUESTIONS TO ASK THE SELLER-AGENT

Are There Any Problems with Neighbors about Overhanging Tree Branches or Roots? ☐ yes ☐ no

Trees whose branches lean over into a neighbor's yard can be a bone of contention as long as you own the property. Roots are a similar problem. You may need to remove the trees to get rid of the problem.

Has Anyone Demanded the Removal of a "Living Fence"? ☐ yes ☐ no

Living fences are growing trees that form a wall at the periphery of the yard. CC&Rs or homeowner organization rules often prohibit living fences above a certain height, typically 5 or 6 feet. Check the rules and the CC&Rs. You may be required to remove them if you buy the home, reducing the privacy of your yard and adding extra expense to the purchase price that you did not plan on.

Are There Any Problems with Roots in Sewer Lines? ☐ yes ☐ no

Tree roots may clog up a sewer line every few months. But, if it isn't happening when you see the property, you won't know about it. If the owner says there is a problem, identify it and negotiate with the owner over a permanent fix. If the seller says there's no problem, get it in writing so that if a chronic plugged line turns up later, you've got recourse against the seller.

Fences and Walls

QUESTIONS TO ASK YOURSELF

Is the Property Completely Fenced? ☐ yes ☐ no

In the western part of the United States, it's considered necessary to fence a lot. If yours isn't fenced, you'll have to pay to have it fenced, at around $1000 to $5000, depending on the type of fence, lot size, and difficulty of terrain. On the East Coast and in the Midwest, fences are not used as much, so a lot without one may not be a problem.

Will You Want Additional Fencing? ☐ yes ☐ no

For privacy you may want an unfenced portion of the yard fenced in. Keep in mind that the current cost is around $10 to $20 a foot for a basic wooden fence, installed. The price is much higher for brick, stone, or cement.

If There's a Pool, Is It Adequately Fenced?

☐ yes   ☐ no

All pools should be completely fenced to a height of at least 5 feet with a gate that closes automatically. This is to help ensure that no one accidentally falls in (especially small children). An unfenced pool is a serious liability issue for you. I recommend that you not accept possession of a home with an unfenced pool.

If There Is a Wooden Fence, Does It Require Painting?

☐ yes   ☐ no

Wooden fences need to be restained about every other year, repainted about every five years. If not stained or painted, a wooden fence will rapidly deteriorate. If you do the work yourself, there's only the cost of materials, usually a couple of hundred dollars. If you hire it out, it can cost far more.

If There Is a Wooden Fence, Does It Need Straightening?

☐ yes   ☐ no

Is the fence leaning or sagging? A properly installed wood fence will have a vertical support post embedded 18 inches into the ground or more that is anchored in a cement footing, which gives the fence its rigidity and strength. Except where there is exceptional ground movement, this should be sufficient to hold the footings and the fence in place. If the fence leans or sags, it usually means the posts were not properly installed and need work. Fence straightening that involves sinking new posts can cost $5 a foot and $50 per post or more, depending on the problem.

Are There Rotten Posts in a Wooden Fence?

☐ yes   ☐ no

Fence posts should be made of pressure-treated ("green") wood as a first choice, cedar or redwood as a second alternative. Treated lumber resists rot and can last decades. Cedar or redword can last many years. Pine or other woods can rot out rapidly, sometimes within five years of installation. A rotten fence post must be replaced, or the fence will fall down. See above for estimated costs.

Are Any Slats Missing in a Wooden Fence?

☐ yes   ☐ no

The most obvious symptom of a fence in poor condition is missing boards. If the fence is otherwise in good shape (posts and runners), the missing boards can usually be replaced for just the cost of the wood and a few minutes spent hammering them in place. But, remember to stain or paint the fence afterward.

Does a Brick or Stone Wall Have Missing Pieces?

☐ yes   ☐ no

Sometimes the top row of bricks or stone will be broken or missing, creating an unsightly appearance. These can easily be replaced, *if* you can find matching materials. If the wall is more than five years old, however, you may have trouble with the match, meaning any repair will look unsightly. A solution might be to replace the fence or to paint it. If large chunks of a brick or stone wall are missing, investigate why they are missing (ground movement, vandalism, bad construction, etc.).

Does a Brick or Cement Wall Need Straightening?

As with a wood fence, the key to a masonry wall is the post. It should be sunk at least 18 inches into the ground and a substantial footer of cement used. If this was not done, or there is significant ground movement, the fence may lean. A leaning masonry wall often cannot be saved; it will tend to crack and break from attempts at straightening it. It may be cheaper simply to tear it down and start over. Masonry walls can cost $35 a running foot and up, depending on width, height, and difficulty of terrain.

Does a Brick or Cement Wall Need Painting?

☐ yes   ☐ no

Painting a brick or cement wall is similar to painting a home. Old paint may need to be removed and several coats of a good paint applied. It can cost $1000 or more to paint a long wall, if done properly.

If There's a Metal Fence, Are All the Pieces in Place?

☐ yes   ☐ no

Fixing a metal fence may require weaving links, welding posts, or bolting sections together. Get an estimate from a metal fence company, as the cost for this type of work varies enormously.

If There Is a Metal Fence, Are There Any Signs of Rust?

☐ yes   ☐ no

Rust is a metal fence's biggest enemy. If there's only surface rust, it can easily be cleaned off and the area painted for protection. Deep rust often hides corroded metal, which must be replaced. If rust is present where a metal post touches the ground or is connected to the cement footing, it could be serious because it indicates that the post could soon fail.

Are All Gates in Good Shape?   ☐ yes   ☐ no

Gates are meant to keep people out and should have the ability to lock. The gate should swing freely on its hinges. Backyard and pool gates should be spring loaded so that after opening, they automatically close on their own.

QUESTIONS TO ASK THE SELLER-AGENT

Is a Peripheral Fence on the Actual Property Line?   ☐ yes   ☐ no

The tendency is to assume that any peripheral fence is on the property line. It may not be. It could be in the neighbor's yard or inside the subject property's yard. If the peripheral fence is *not* on the property line, you'll need to get a plot plan to see just where the boundaries really are.

Have There Been Any Disputes with Neighbors over the Location of a Fence?   ☐ yes   ☐ no

Boundary disputes can be long lasting and intractable. If there is a fence dispute (typically over location, height, or type), demand that it be resolved *before* you conclude the purchase. If you don't, you'll inherit the problem . . . and possibly legal fees involved in resolving it.

Does the Height of the Fence Comply with CC&Rs?

☐ yes ☐ no

Typically the CC&Rs or homeowner's association rules will limit the height of fences. Is a fence or wall in noncompliance? Has a neighbor or the HOA asked that it be removed or lowered? If so, it should be taken care of before the purchase is completed. Demand to see the CC&Rs and rules yourself.

Has Anyone Ever Asked and/or Demanded that a Fence Be Removed?

☐ yes ☐ no

If they have and the issue has not been resolved, you could be faced with having to remedy a difficult problem. And that problem could come to a head in a lawsuit. Thoroughly investigate whenever a seller says that someone has demanded that a fence be removed, repaired, or changed. It could be a problem that is sufficiently serious to keep you from buying the property.

Drainage

QUESTIONS TO ASK YOURSELF

Is the Home Higher or Lower Than the Street Level?

☐ yes ☐ no

Ideally, the home will be higher than the street in front. That way water will run off into the street. (Normally, for good drainage, water flows from back to front in a yard.) If the house is lower than the street, or the backyard is lower than the front, water can collect in the yard and come into the home during the rainy season.

Are There Any Water Blockages in the Side Yards?

☐ yes ☐ no

Piles of wood, sand, dirt, garbage, or other refuse can block the normal drainage of water from the backyard to the street, causing flooding. Removing the debris will solve the problem for the future, but won't correct damage already done. Have it professionally evaluated.

Are There Any Depressions in the Yards?

☐ yes ☐ no

Small sinkholes indicate a water problem, even if there is no water present at the time. A drain installed at the bottom of the sinkhole indicates that a cure has been attempted. Putting in a drain where there is none can cost as much as several thousand dollars.

Is There Any Standing Water?

☐ yes ☐ no

There should never be any water standing in puddles in the yard. If you see some when you visit, be sure to get a soils and drainage inspection report to help determine how severe the problem may be.

Are There Gutters on the Home?

☐ yes ☐ no

Unlike what most of us suppose, the main purpose of gutters is not to keep us from getting wet when we walk into a home. The main purpose of gutters is to divert rainwater away from the home and foundation. Proper gutters have intact drainpipes, often with drain tubes at the bottom leading water away from the house. It can cost upward of $2000 or more to install a complete gutter system.

QUESTIONS TO ASK THE SELLER-AGENT

Is the Home in a Floodplain?

☐ yes   ☐ no

Even if the seller or agent says no, ask for a district report on flood-plains, available through the title insurance company. If the property is located in a floodplain, getting insurance will be more difficult and costly. It also means that sometimes your home could be in peril from flooding rivers or other water sources.

If Near a Shore, Is the Home Subject to High Tides or Other Flooding?

☐ yes   ☐ no

Just because a river, lake, or stream is 200 feet away when you look at the property, that doesn't mean it will always stay that far away. Again, even if the seller says no, ask for any district reports. Sometimes it is not possible to get any insurance on homes that are subject to occasional tidal flooding.

Are There Any Streams Leading into the Property?

☐ yes   ☐ no

In certain cases before a tract of houses was built, a stream meandered through the undeveloped property. Don't be fooled because the home is in the middle of a tract of houses. Streams can come back to life during rainy periods and periodically flood nearby basements and homes.

Are There Any Underground Water Problems?

☐ yes   ☐ no

Sometimes the water table is very high, meaning that during a rainy season the water may come up out of the ground artesian-style. Be sure to check the foundation for watermarks from previous flooding as well as question the seller and/or agent.

Any There Any Water Problems During the Rainy Season?   ☐ yes   ☐ no

This is a catch-all question that covers a host of ills from groundwater to streams to flooding to anything else. If a seller denies any problems, get it in writing. If it later turns out there is a chronic water problem that the seller knew about (or should have known about), you will have a better case.

Are There Any French Drains?   ☐ yes   ☐ no

These are designed to absorb and carry away water that would otherwise create a problem. A working French drain system can handle an enormous amount of water flow. Ask where the drain is, why it was installed, and if it works efficiently.

Is There a Sump Pump? Why?   ☐ yes   ☐ no

Usually a sump pump is used when there is no other alternative. In most homes, the slope of the land will carry water away. If the house is in a hole, or otherwise does not have adequate drainage, a sump pump may have to be used. Ask about the location, the purpose for its installation, and whether it was installed with a building department permit. (If not, ask the seller to bring it up to code.)

Sewer and/or Septic

QUESTIONS TO ASK YOURSELF

Is the Property Connected to a Municipal Sewer System?

☐ **yes** ☐ **no**

Ideally the home you are considering will have a waste disposal system hooked directly into a municipal sewer. Waste solids and water are carried away. A less efficient system, often found in rural areas, is a septic system.

Is There a Septic System?

☐ **yes** ☐ **no**

A septic system allows waste materials to be disposed of on your own property. It consists of three basic elements: a leach field, which handle liquids; a septic tank in which solids decompose; and the pipes necessary to connect them to the home. A septic system needs to be cleaned out periodically (every five years or so) and the cleaning cost is typically around $300 (including fees for toxic dumping). If properly constructed and maintained, it can last indefinitely.

Are There Any Odors from the System?

☐ **yes** ☐ **no**

Odors from either a municipal sewer or a septic system are not normal and indicate problems. These can usually be smelled at the side of the house, or sometimes inside. When you smell odors, you should insist on a complete inspection of the home's waste disposal system.

Is It Functioning When You See the Property?

☐ yes   ☐ no

The municipal sewer or septic system should be functioning when you see the home. If you flush the toilet several times and the water doesn't go down, there could be a problem either in the pipes or in the septic system (if there is one). Again, have a thorough inspection of the system.

Is There a Pump?

☐ yes   ☐ no

A septic system's leach field needs to be quite large—on the order of 20 by 40 feet. Sometimes the only good location for it is uphill from the house. This requires a septic pump to move liquid waste uphill to the leach field. Sometimes a pump is required to boost both solid and liquid waste uphill to a municipal sewer system. If there's a pump, be sure to have it inspected for wear and efficiency.

QUESTIONS TO ASK THE SELLER-AGENT

Are There Any Sewer Assessment Bonds on the Property?

☐ yes   ☐ no

When a home is connected to a municipal sewer system (whether new or resale), there is normally a public bond floated to cover the cost of bringing the system to the home. This is assessed to the property. In new homes, builders normally pay off the assessment. In older home connects, sometimes the bond is paid off over time. If there is a bond, it is customary to demand that the seller pay it off prior to the close of escrow.

What Is the Annual Sewer Assessment?

yes no

Sometimes called a "toilet tax," municipalities charge for maintaining the public sewer pipes, including waste disposal plants. These fees can be substantial, running from a low of about $15 a toilet to a high of several hundred dollars. Find out if there is a fee, what it is, and how it will impact your monthly payments.

Where Is the Leach Field (Septic System)?

yes no

You cannot build on or pave over a leach field. You will want to limit what you grow over a leach field to plants with short root systems. Therefore, it is a good idea to have the seller point out where the leach field is. The seller may not know, particularly if he or she is not the original owner; however, county records should reveal this information.

Is There Room for a Secondary Leach Field (Septic System)?

yes no

If the septic tank is not cleaned out often enough, solid wastes may travel into the liquid-dispensing pipes of the leach field, plugging them. When this happens, a new leach field in a different location must be created. New homes usually have room designated for a secondary field; sometimes older homes do not. Be sure that if the property has a septic system, it has room for a secondary field. If no new field can be installed, the home could be condemned! Installing a leach field costs around $2500 and up, which is a good reason to have the septic tank cleaned often.

Are There Any Problems with the Sewer Line?

yes   no

Leaks, plugs from tree roots, improper operation because of bad construction—all can be serious and expensive problems to cure. Ask the seller if he or she has had to call out a plumber in the last five years to clean the sewer system. If so, ask to see the receipts, which should have the problem and the cure written on them. (Homeowners typically keep all home-related documents forever.)

How Old Is Any Pump or Other Mechanical Equipment?

yes   no

A sewer pump, sump pump, or other equipment associated with the waste disposal system does not last forever. Most have a life span of between 10 and 15 years. If the equipment is already 10 years old or older, expect it to fail soon. Replacing a sewer pump can cost between $500 and $1000. If it is working, you cannot normally expect the seller to pay this cost.

Pool and Spa

QUESTIONS TO ASK YOURSELF

Are the Pool and Spa Large Enough?

yes   no

Sometimes they are little more than a pond. A spa should be large enough to easily hold four adults, and a pool should be large enough for the kids to splash around in and for adults to do laps. A pool that is smaller than that tends to look ridiculous and is more a liability than an asset.

Is the Water Clear?

☐ yes ☐ no

Contamination is the biggest problem with existing pools. Crystal-clear water suggests that the filter is working and that appropriate chemicals have been added. Murky water indicates problems, and you should have a pool service evaluate the water.

Are the Walls of the Pool Discolored?

☐ yes ☐ no

Too much or too little acid in the water can discolor walls, as can chemicals normally occurring in water over time. The only way to clean them is to drain the pool (which can only be done when the groundwater level is low—usually in summer) and either replaster or acid wash. An acid wash (which can only be done several times during the life of a pool) costs several hundred dollars. Figure $5000 and up for replastering.

Are Any Tiles Missing?

☐ yes ☐ no

The installation cost of a few replacement tiles is minimal, typically under $100. Finding tile to match, however, can be a problem.

Is There Any Yellow or Green Algae?

☐ yes ☐ no

Lack of chlorination and ineffective filtering cause algae to form. Yellow and/or green algae can usually be quickly removed by scrubbing, super-chlorinating, and changing the filter. A service can do this for $50 to $75 as long as the problem is not severe.

Is There Any Black Algae?

If not treated in time, yellow or green algae can turn to black algae, which can eat into the plaster. Black algae can usually be removed by scrubbing or, in severe cases, by acid washing and then replastering (see above). Removing black algae by scrubbing can cost several hundred dollars. Be sure the seller takes care of this.

Does All the Pool Equipment Work?

☐ yes   ☐ no

When you turn on the pump, the water should immediately circulate through it and the filter and back into the pool. A high reading on the pump pressure gauge indicates the filter is clogged and needs cleaning. Have the seller take care of it. Recheck after the maintenance work is done to be sure the pressure is down.

Does the Spa Have High-Pressure Air and Water?

☐ yes   ☐ no

A well-designed spa will have both. Some older spas are just like bathtubs, no bubbles, only hot water. There should be separate switches and pumps for both the high-pressure air and water. If they are not built into the spa, it can cost thousands to have them retrofitted.

Does the Heater Work?

☐ yes   ☐ no

The spa and/or pool heater should have separate on-off and temperature switches. When the heater is turned on, you should be able to feel the heat instantly on the pipe that leads out from the heater. If you don't feel significant heat on the output, it indicates that the heater is clogged or defective. Have a pool service check it. A new pool heater can easily cost $1500.

How Old Is the Heater?

☐ **yes**   ☐ **no**

Newer heaters are nearly three times more efficient than older ones. Plan on extra fuel costs for any heater that is more than 10 years old. Old heaters, however, if properly maintained, can last almost indefinitely.

Are the Motors Noisy?

☐ **yes**   ☐ **no**

All pool motors tend to make noise. But excessive noise, particularly any high-pitched whines, suggests that the motor may be burning out. Figure around $250 for a new pump motor, plus installation.

Is the Pool Filter Large Enough?

☐ **yes**   ☐ **no**

Too often a small filter is installed to save money. However, it will be ineffective. A diatomaceous earth filter is considered the best. Check with a pool service to see if the filter has enough filtering area for the pool and/or spa. A new filter can cost between $200 and $500.

QUESTIONS TO ASK THE SELLER-AGENT

Are There Any Problems with the Pool or Spa?

☐ **yes**   ☐ **no**

Be *very* suspicious of any "No" answer. This is an area that always has problems. Have a pool service check out any stated difficulties.

Who Is Your Pool and/or Spa Maintenance Person? ☐ yes ☐ no

Call him or her. Ask for a complete breakdown on the pool or spa, including any problems that were dealt with, as well as the estimates to get them properly fixed. Have the seller make the corrections.

Garage and/or Carport

QUESTIONS TO ASK YOURSELF

Is There Enough Room for All Your Vehicles? ☐ yes ☐ no

Usually the bigger the garage, the better. A three-car garage is preferred by almost everyone, even if just for the extra storage space. If you have three vehicles and settle for a one- or two-car garage, you'll have to park some of your vehicles in the driveway or on the street all the time. Expanding the garage is usually prohibitively expensive, so you may want to consider a different home with a bigger garage.

Is There Enough Room for Storage? ☐ yes ☐ no

Few houses have enough storage space, which is why the garage becomes the big storage room. An oversized garage with storage space is a huge plus. If the garage is too small for your needs, you might have to rent a locker elsewhere for your extras.

What About a Work Space?

☐ yes   ☐ no

It's convenient to have a workbench, even a small one, in a garage. It usually requires a space of at least 2 feet by 4 feet. If there isn't even that much room, and you're a handyperson, will you be satisfied with the house?

Are Any Leaks Evident?

☐ yes   ☐ no

Check walls and ceilings for watermarks. If there are signs of leaks, have a roofing contractor check out the roof. Often a garage will have a separate roof from the home. Get an estimate of costs and replacement and be sure to negotiate with the seller to pay all or some of the cost.

Is the Garage Insulated?

☐ yes   ☐ no

Most garages are not. Yet even in moderate climates, garages can be too cold or hot to work in. Getting the garage insulated will cost several hundred dollars, provided you do not have the walls and/or ceiling sheetrocked, which can cost several hundred more.

Is There a Garage Door Opener? Does It Work?

☐ yes   ☐ no

Today this is considered a necessity. Try it out through several cycles. It should have a safety feature that reverses direction if it encounters any resistance (such as a small child!). A garage door opener costs under $200 plus another $100 for installation.

Is There a Sink in the Garage?

☐ yes   ☐ no

This is not a necessity, but it can be a real plus for cleaning up after you've been working on vehicles or outside. It is very difficult and expensive to retrofit, particularly the installation of drain lines.

7
Layout, Color, and Design

The Front of the House

QUESTIONS TO ASK YOURSELF

Does It Look Good?   ☐ yes   ☐ no

"Curb appeal" is how the home looks when you first drive up. If all the features combined make it look good, it's probably a house that you may like, and that will resell later quickly and for more money. Stay away from, or plan to change, homes with poor curb appeal.

Is the Home Well Situated on Its Lot?   ☐ yes   ☐ no

It should have a pleasant appearance similar to that of other neighboring homes. If placed at an awkward angle, or too far back on the lot, or with a side facing the street, the value of the home will suffer. You may pay less to buy, but you'll get less when you resell.

Is It on a Busy Street or in a Cul-de-Sac?

☐ yes   ☐ no

People prefer quiet streets with little traffic—a cul-de-sac, or small dead-end street, is usually the best. A home on a corner lot that faces two heavily trafficked streets is the worst location. (A corner lot is usually larger, but the added space is often wasted in the front.)

Is the Lot Large Enough?

☐ yes   ☐ no

Most people like a big lot for privacy, but want a small lot for low maintenance. Overly large or very small lots can be a problem when it comes time to resell. Always be sure the lot is large enough to satisfy your family's needs.

Is the Home Large Enough?

☐ yes   ☐ no

Are there enough bedrooms to accommodate your family? Is there enough square footage to give "room to roam"? Three bedrooms with two baths are considered minimum for a modern home. Many small bedrooms are considered to be a detracting feature, as are small living areas.

Is the House a Modern Color?

☐ yes   ☐ no

Housing colors have changed dramatically in the last 10 years; preferred colors have become lighter. Houses painted dark browns and greens tend to be passé. Repainting the outside of the home can easily cost $2500.

Is the Color Appropriate for the Home? □ yes □ no

Obviously a bright purple house is going to stand out like a sore thumb. However, a Spanish-style home that is painted green will look equally strange. Or a Cape Cod that is painted brown. The color should complement the style of the home, and it should look new and fresh.

Is the Trim a Good Accent Color? □ yes □ no

Trim should almost always be a complementary color. It should be pleasing to the eye. Also, all the trim areas (window and door moldings, trim boards, and so on) should be painted the color of the trim, not the major color of the house.

Is There a Third Accent Color for the Doors and/or Windows? □ yes □ no

In a well-thought-out color scheme, a third accent color will often be used for the front door and a few other select areas. If done correctly, it will greatly add to the appeal of the home.

Is the Design in Keeping with the Area? □ yes □ no

A New England cottage will look awkward among Spanish ranch-style homes. So will a colonial look out of place among Tudor-style properties. The home's design should blend with the neighborhood norms; otherwise, it will be the ugly duckling that's always hard to resell.

Is the Design Convincing?

☐ yes   ☐ no

Some homes look ridiculous as a result of the failed attempts by a designer to make them stylish. Fake columns pretending to be Roman pillars, a forced façade trying to give the impression of a plantation style, or other embellishments that don't work can make the home, and neighborhood, unattractive. You probably will want to pass, as will future buyers.

Are the Doors (Garage and Front) Modern?

☐ yes   ☐ no

This is what people tend to look at first and if they're old or deteriorated, they can detract from the home's value. A new garage door can easily cost $1000. A new front door can cost anywhere from $500 to $5000. These are typically not costs that the seller will pay for.

Does the Landscaping Fit the Home?

☐ yes   ☐ no

Tall pine, cypress, or palm trees next to a one-story home tend to make it look squat. Tree removal can cost upward of $500 apiece. Junipers as hedges are considered to be out of style and can likewise be expensive to remove. If you're not sure, consult a landscape architect to tell you how well the landscaping fits, and how much it will cost to upgrade it.

The Living Areas

QUESTIONS TO ASK YOURSELF

Does It Feel Right?

☐ yes   ☐ no

You should pass on the home if the living areas are awkward and don't feel comfortable. Or, if they detract from the home to the point where it will be difficult for you to resell. Look especially for the items below.

Is There an Entry?

☐ yes   ☐ no

Every quality house, even a small one, will have a separate entryway or hallway. This is where you welcome guests and they get their first view of the home. Homes that simply open into the living room are considered awkward.

Are the Sight Lines Pleasant?

☐ yes   ☐ no

Sight lines are what you see from various positions in the home. When you enter, do you see the living room couch or the bathroom toilet? From the dining room, do you see the kitchen or the garbage cans outside? Good sight lines make for a good house.

Do the Rooms Flow Well?

☐ yes   ☐ no

Moving from room to room should seem natural and make sense. Avoid homes that move from bedroom to living room or from kitchen to bathroom. Kitchens should be near dining rooms, family rooms should be isolated (to cut down on the noise to the bedrooms), and bathrooms and utility rooms should be convenient to bedrooms.

Are There Any Awkward Angles or Dark Corners?   ☐ yes   ☐ no

A long hallway between the entry and the kitchen, or a dark living room can detract enormously from a home. Good design will make each room light and airy without long hallways. An unexpected turn into a bedroom or bathroom is another giveaway of a badly designed home.

Do Windows and Doors Match the Home's Décor?   ☐ yes   ☐ no

Window grids (as in French windows) don't belong on a Spanish-style home. An elegant oak door can look awkward on a small cottage. The style of the windows and doors should not overshadow or diminish the style of the home.

The Kitchen

QUESTIONS TO ASK YOURSELF

Is the Kitchen Modern?   ☐ yes   ☐ no

Every buyer wants a modern kitchen. Any kitchen that is over 10 years old and has not been renovated can be considered old-fashioned. A minor kitchen renovation can cost $10,000; a major one can cost upward of $50,000. You may want to subtract this amount from the price you offer the seller.

Is It Large Enough?

☐ **yes**　　☐ **no**

Today people want a kitchen with enough space for several worksta-
tions plus an eating area. The old, large farm-style kitchen has made a
comeback. Homes with small kitchens are less valued. Adding space to
a kitchen can be very difficult and extremely expensive—better to buy
a home with a kitchen that is already large enough.

Does It Have Enough Shelf Space?

☐ **yes**　　☐ **no**

Generally speaking, the more cabinets the better. Adding cabinets can
be expensive, since you'll probably want to replace all, as matching old
to new may be impossible. Kitchen cabinets can easily cost $10,000.

Do the Countertops Match the Home's Standards?

☐ **yes**　　☐ **no**

You expect granite countertops in an elegant home and tile or Formica
in a more modest setting. Beware of homes that are overbuilt with
countertops that are far more expensive than the home deserves. Don't
pay more for the house because someone wasted money putting in a
kitchen that is too fancy.

Do the Floors Match the Home's Standards?

☐ **yes**　　☐ **no**

Marble floors are elegant in a fancy house, out of place in a small cottage. Wood floors in the kitchen look wonderful, until water spills and
they warp. The kitchen floors should match the needs of the kitchen
and the style of the home. It can easily cost $1000 to $5000 to replace a
kitchen floor.

Is It Clean? □ yes □ no

You expect the kitchen to be clean, especially the stove and other appliances. If not, for a couple of hundred dollars a cleaning crew can come in and make the place spotless. Just be sure dirt isn't covering up problems.

The Master Bedroom and Bath

QUESTIONS TO ASK YOURSELF

Does the Master Bedroom Face the Street? □ yes □ no

The master bedroom should not face the street, or you'll be bothered by street noise all night long. Ideally, it should face the back. You may want to pass on a house with a front-facing master bedroom; it's that important.

Is the Master Bedroom Large Enough? □ yes □ no

Modern homes have large master bedrooms. Older homes tended to have smaller ones. Today's buyers look for a huge master bedroom. You'll have trouble reselling with a small one.

Is It Airy?

☐ **yes**   ☐ **no**

There should be many windows and/or skylights in the master bed-room. A dark master bedroom can be salvaged by adding skylights, but at a cost of $200 to $1000 apiece. (Don't expect the seller to pick up the tab.)

Is There a Bathroom off the Master Bedroom?

☐ **yes**   ☐ **no**

This is a necessity in a modern home. If not, plan on adding it. The cost could easily be $10,000 to $25,000. You may want to pass on a house that does not have this feature, as it will be difficult to resell.

Is the Master Bath Large Enough?

☐ **yes**   ☐ **no**

Modern homes have very large master bathrooms. Typically they have double sinks as well as both a tub and a separate shower. A large bath-room here is a plus, a small one a minus, particularly when it comes time to resell.

Does It Have a Whirlpool Tub?

☐ **yes**   ☐ **no**

This is not a necessity, but can be a real plus. Retrofitting a whirlpool tub can cost $500 for the tub itself and anywhere from $1500 to $10,000, depending on the difficulties involved in the installation.

Do the Master Bedroom and Bath Flow Together? ☐ yes   ☐ no

There should be a natural connection. There should also be a door between the master bedroom and bath; this is sometimes not done in modern homes to make the space look bigger. (You need to be able to close off the bathroom space so that someone using it at night or early in the morning doesn't disturb another person trying to sleep in the bedroom.)

Is There Enough Closet Space? ☐ yes   ☐ no

Walk-in closets are preferred, although any closet space is desirable. Organizers in the form of built-in drawers in the closets are highly desirable, but do not add to the price of the home in most buyers' eyes.

The Backyard

QUESTIONS TO ASK YOURSELF

Is the Backyard Large Enough? Too Large? Is There Room to Expand? ☐ yes   ☐ no

A huge backyard may be just what you want for your kids, but because of maintenance considerations, it may make reselling more difficult. Try to balance your immediate needs with the appeal to a future buyer.

Is the Landscaping Adequate?   ☐ yes   ☐ no

Fully landscaped rear yards are a plus, but don't pay extra for them. Most people figure they can fix up the backyard themselves over time.

Will the Yard Require a Lot of Maintenance?   ☐ yes   ☐ no

Will you be willing to do the work? Lawns need mowing and are best avoided, unless you want them for their looks and play area. A sprinkler or drip system will help (costs about $200 to $2000 to install, depending on size and coverage). Shrubs, bushes, and trees provide shade and require only occasional trimming.

Is There a Deck and/or Overhang?   ☐ yes   ☐ no

A deck or overhang is a real plus, but don't pay extra for them. You can build a deck or overhang for between $1000 and $5000, depending on size.

Is There a Pool or Spa?   ☐ yes   ☐ no

An aboveground spa can cost $5000; one that is below ground can cost $10,000. Even a small pool can cost $25,000. However, while these can add to the desirability of the home, they seldom add as much as they cost to the price. Don't pay a lot more for a home that has these features.

Is There RV Access?   ☐ yes   ☐ no

This is very important to some people and a real plus. Some buyers will only purchase homes with space on the side or back for their RV. It can help when it's time to resell.

8

Other Considerations

Neighborhood

QUESTIONS TO ASK YOURSELF

Should I Avoid Buying in Certain Areas?

☐ yes   ☐ no

Your goal should be to buy in the very best neighborhood you can. Further, even if you like the property, if the neighborhood has detracting features (noted below), you may want to look in a different neighborhood. The better quality neighborhood you buy into, the faster your home will increase in value and the quicker it will resell.

Have You Heard Good Things about the Neighborhood?

☐ yes ☐ no

Chances are friends, acquaintances, or real-estate agents have told you about different neighborhoods. Is this one they praised, condemned, or were so-so about? A neighborhood's reputation helps determine how high a price you'll pay when you buy—and perhaps more important, how quickly and how much the house will appreciate when you own it. The better the neighborhood, the more money you stand to make over time. The best thing you can do with a bad neighborhood is pass on it.

Are the Lawns All Mowed, the Houses Neat, Clean, and Painted?

☐ yes ☐ no

Look at the neighboring houses on this and nearby streets. You want to see well-cared-for properties indicating pride of ownership. Any unkempt lawns or other eyesores mean that there are problems in the neighborhood . . . and you may want to look elsewhere.

Is There Any Graffiti?

☐ yes ☐ no

This is a sign of gang activity and lack of owner pride. In a good neighborhood, there will be no graffiti or, if any goes up, it will be immediately removed. You'll have trouble reselling in a neighborhood that has graffiti.

Are There Any Trash Cans Out or Trash on Lawns or on the Street?

☐ yes ☐ no

In a proud neighborhood (or one with a strong homeowner's association), trash cans will be put out only on pickup day and then immediately removed. Cans laying around suggest neighborhood problems, and you may want to look elsewhere.

Are There Lots of Kids Around?

☐ yes   ☐ no

This is good if you have children and are looking for them to have playmates. This is bad if you are retired and want a quiet community in which to live. Check the ages of the kids to be sure they match yours.

Are People Working on Cars in Their Driveways and on Lawns?

☐ yes   ☐ no

This is not unusual on a Saturday morning. But at other times there should be no sign of such work. Cars in various states of repair left in driveways, on lawns, or on the street indicate a lack of pride in the area and is unsightly, which can depress real estate values.

What's the Crime Rate?

☐ yes   ☐ no

Check with the community representative of the local police department. These statistics are broken down by types of crime and by block. You may want to pass on a high-crime neighborhood.

How Are the Schools?

☐ yes   ☐ no

Schools are the single most important factor in determining price appreciation. Good schools mean profits for homeowners. Substandard schools mean that you will have difficulty reselling and getting your price.

Pests

QUESTIONS TO ASK YOURSELF

Are You Having a Pest Inspection?
☐ yes   ☐ no

Normally to get any new financing, you'll need a termite and pest inspection. If you're paying cash (or, for some reason, the lender doesn't require this), get it yourself. Normally the seller pays to get a termite and pest clearance, which includes the inspection and any work required to remove the pests and repair any damage.

Do You See Any Signs of Termite Infestation?
☐ yes   ☐ no

Look for signs as you tour the property; you can later ask the pest inspector about these. Small amounts of detritus around the periphery of the home (inside and out) suggest termites. Mud tunnels on the foundation or under the house also suggest termites. Large black ants walking around the house suggest carpenter ants, which can be just as destructive as termites.

Is There Any Black Mold?
☐ yes   ☐ no

This mold is typically damp and, in severe cases, the mold is actually raised off the surface off the wood. While probably not dangerous, some people are allergic to its spores, so don't get too close. Removal can be very expensive. Be sure to later point this out to the pest inspector and to have the seller take care of it.

Is There Any Wood Rot?

☐ yes ☐ no

Called dry rot, it actually occurs when moisture is allowed to come in contact with wood. The wood seems to disintegrate. You can tell by poking beams, joists, wallboards, or anything else with a screwdriver. They should be resistive and solid. If the screwdriver sinks in, you could have a problem. (I usually mark the spot with a piece of chalk so it can easily be found later on.)

Are There Any Spiders?

☐ yes ☐ no

In some parts of the country black widow spiders are common. In other areas brown recluse spiders pose problems. Yet in other areas, scorpions are found. All are dangerous. If you see spider webs, be careful. Also, do not turn over loose pieces of wood in a basement, as you may not like what's hidden underneath. Mention any concerns to the pest inspector.

Is Anything Else Suspicious?

☐ yes ☐ no

Even if you've never looked under a home before, you can often tell if something is amiss simply because things won't look right. Note any potential problems and bring them up later with a professional. Better to ask a dumb question than to overlook something important.

QUESTIONS TO ASK THE SELLER-AGENT

Are There Any Pest Problems?

☐ yes   ☐ no

Pest problems can run the gamut from spiders to termites to rodents. Usually an exterminator of one sort or another was called. This means there was a report as well as an invoice. Ask the seller to produce these. (Sellers usually keep all this information.) Have a professional home inspector later review the paperwork.

How Were the Problems Corrected? When?

☐ yes   ☐ no

The invoice should indicate what was done and how long ago. Keep in mind that extermination work is short lived. A termite colony that has been removed could reestablish itself in as little as 90 days (although the pest removal company usually gives a guarantee for 180 to 360 days). Any work done more than six months ago should not be considered current.

Who Is Going to Do the Pest and/or Termite Inspection?

☐ yes   ☐ no

Since the seller pays for it, the seller normally chooses. Find out who it will be (or ask to be told before the inspector comes out). That way you can call and ask the inspector to check on anything you found.

Glossary

Terms You Need to Understand

If you're just getting introduced to real estate, you'll quickly realize that people in this field have a language all their own. There are *points* and *disclosures* and *contingencies* and dozens of other terms that can make you think people are talking in a foreign language.

Since buying a home is one of the biggest financial decisions in life, it's a good idea to become familiar with the following terms, which are frequently used in real estate. All too often a lack of understanding can result in very real consequences such as confusion and failure to act (or inappropriate action) on an important issue.

Abstract of Title: A written document produced by a title insurance company (in some states an attorney will do it) giving the history of who owned the property from the first owner forward. It also indicates any liens or encumbrances that may affect the title. A lender will not make a loan, nor can a sale normally conclude, until the title to real estate is clear, as evidenced by the abstract.

Acceleration Clause: A clause that "accelerates" the payments in a mortgage, meaning that the entire amount becomes immediately due and payable. Most mortgages contain this clause (which kicks in if, for example, you sell the property).

Adjustable Rate Mortgage (ARM): A mortgage whose interest rate fluctuates according to an index and a margin agreed to in advance by borrower and lender.

Adjustment Date: The day on which an adjustment is made in an adjustable rate mortgage. It may occur monthly, every six months, once a year, or as otherwise agreed.

Agent: Any person licensed to sell real estate, whether a broker or a salesperson.

Alienation Clause: A clause in a mortgage specifying that if the property is transferred to another person, the mortgage becomes immediately due and payable. *See also* Acceleration Clause.

ALTA: American Land Title Association. A more complete and extensive policy of title insurance and one that most lenders insist upon. It involves a physical inspection and often guarantees the property's boundaries. Lenders often insist on an ALTA policy, with themselves named as beneficiary.

Amortization: Paying back the mortgage in equal installments. In other words, if the mortgage is for 30 years, you pay in 360 equal installments. (The last payment is often a few dollars more or less. This is the opposite of a Balloon Payment, which is a payment that is considerably larger than the rest.) *See* Balloon Payment.

Annual Percentage Rate (APR): The rate paid for a loan, including interest, loan fees, and points. As determined by a government formula.

Appraisal: Valuation of a property, usually by a qualified appraiser, as required by most lenders. The amount of the appraisal is the maximum value on which the loan will be based. For example, if the appraisal is $100,000 and the lender loans 80 percent of value, the maximum mortgage will be $80,000.

ASA: American Society of Appraisers. A professional organization of appraisers.

As Is: A property sold without warrantees from the sellers. The sellers are essentially saying that they won't make any repairs.

Assignment of Mortgage: The lender's sale of a mortgage usually without the borrower's permission. For example, you may obtain a mortgage from XYZ Savings and Loan, which then sells the mortgage to Bland Bank. You will get a letter saying that the mortgage was assigned and you are to make your payments to a new entity. The document used between lenders for the transfer is the "assignment of mortgage."

Assumption: Taking over an existing mortgage. For example, a seller may have an assumable mortgage on a property. When you buy the property, you take over that seller's obligation under the loan. Today most fixed rate mortgages are not assumable. Most adjustable rate mortgages are assumable, but the borrower must qualify. FHA and VA mortgages may be assumable if certain conditions are met. When you assume the mortgage, you may be personally liable if there is a foreclosure.

Automatic Guarantee: The power assigned to some lenders to guarantee VA loans without first checking with the Veterans Administration. These lenders can often make the loans more quickly.

Backup: An offer that comes in after an earlier offer is accepted. If both buyer and seller agree, the backup assumes a secondary position to be acted upon only if the original deal does not go through.

Balloon Payment: A single mortgage payment, usually the last, that is larger than all the others. In the case of second mortgages held by sellers, often only interest is paid until the due date—then the entire amount borrowed (the principal) is due. *See* Second Mortgage.

Biweekly Mortgage: A mortgage that is paid every other week instead of monthly. Since there are 52 weeks in the year, you end up making 26 payments, or the equivalent of one month's extra payment. The additional payments, applied to the principal, significantly reduce the amount of interest charged on the mortgage and often reduce the term of the loan.

Blanket Mortgage: A mortgage that covers several properties instead of a single mortgage on each property. It is used most frequently by developers and builders.

Broker: An independent licensed agent, one who can establish his or her own office. Salespeople must work for brokers, typically for a few years, to get enough experience to become licensed as brokers.

Buy-Down Mortgage: A mortgage with a lower than market interest rate, either for the entire term of the mortgage or for a set period at the beginning—say, two years. The buy-down is made possible by the builder or seller paying an up-front fee to the lender.

Buyer's Agent: A real estate agent whose loyalty is to the buyer and not to the seller. Such agents are becoming increasingly common today.

Call Provision: A clause in a mortgage allowing the lender to call in the entire unpaid balance of the loan providing certain events have occurred, such as sale of the property. *See also* Acceleration Clause.

Canvass: To work a neighborhood, to go through it, and knock on every door. Agents canvass to find listings. Investors and home buyers do it to find potential sellers who have not yet listed their property—and may agree to sell quickly for less.

Caps: Limits put on an adjustable rate mortgage. The interest rate, the monthly payment, or both may be capped.

CC&Rs: Covenants, conditions, and restrictions These limit the activities you as an owner may do. For example, you may be required to seek approval of a Home Owners' Association before adding on or changing the color of your house. Or you may be restricted from adding a second or third story to your home.

Certificate of Reasonable Value (CRV): A document issued by the Veterans Administration establishing what the VA feels is the property's maximum value. In some cases, if a buyer pays more than this amount for the property, he or she will not get the VA loan.

Chain of Title: The history of ownership of the property. The title to property forms a chain going back to the first owners, which in the Southwest, for example, may come from original Spanish land grants.

Closing: When the seller conveys title to the buyer and the buyer makes full payment, including financing, for the property. At the closing, all required documents are signed and delivered and funds are disbursed.

Commission: The fee charged for an agent's services. Usually, but not always, the seller pays. There is no "set" fee; rather, the amount is fully negotiable.

Commitment: A promise from lender to borrower offering a mortgage at a set amount, interest rate, and cost. Typically, commitments have a time limit—for example, they are good for 5 or 15 days. Some lenders charge for making a commitment if you don't subsequently take out the mortgage (since they have tied up the money for that amount of time). When the lender's offer is in writing, it is sometimes called a "firm commitment."

Conforming Loan: A mortgage that conforms to the underwriting requirements of Fannie Mae or Freddie Mac.

Construction Loan: A mortgage made for the purpose of constructing a building. The loan is short term, typically under 12 months, and is usually paid in installments directly to the builder as the work is completed. Most often, it is interest only.

Contingency: A condition that limits a contract. For example, the most common contingency says that a buyer is not required to complete a purchase if he or she fails to get necessary financing. *See also* Subject To.

Conventional Loan: Any loan that is not guaranteed or insured by the government.

Convertible Mortgage: An adjustable rate mortgage (ARM) with a clause allowing it to be converted to a fixed rate mortgage at some time in the future. You may have to pay an additional cost to obtain this type of mortgage.

Cosigner: Someone with better credit (usually a close relative) who agrees to sign your loan if you do not have good enough credit to qualify for a mortgage. The cosigner is equally responsible for repayment of the loan. (If you don't pay it back, the cosigner can be held liable for the entire balance.)

Credit Report: A report, usually from one of the country's three large credit reporting companies, that gives your credit history. It typically lists all your delinquent payments or failures to pay as well as any bankruptcies and, sometimes, foreclosures. Lenders use the report to determine whether to offer you a mortgage. The fee for obtaining the report is usually under $50, and you are charged for it.

Deal Point: A point on which the deal hinges. It can be as important as the price or as trivial as changing the color of the mailbox.

Deposit: The money that buyers put up (also called "earnest money") to demonstrate their seriousness in making an offer. The deposit is usually at risk if the buyers fail to complete the transaction and have no acceptable way of backing out of the deal.

Disclosures: A list and explanation of features and defects in a property that sellers give to buyers. Most states now require disclosures.

Discount: The amount that a lender withholds from a mortgage to cover the points and fees. For example, you may borrow $100,000, but your points and fees come to $3000; hence the lender will fund only $97,000, discounting the $3000. Also, in the secondary market, a discount is the amount less than face value that a buyer of a mortgage pays in order to be induced to take out the loan. The discount here is calculated on the basis of risk, market rates, interest rate of the note, and other factors. *See* Points.

Dual Agent: An agent who expresses loyalty to both buyers and sellers and agrees to work with both. Only a few agents can successfully play this role.

Due-on-Encumbrance Clause: A little noted and seldom-enforced clause in recent mortgages that allows the lender to foreclose if the borrower gets additional financing. For example, if you secure a second mortgage, the lender of the first mortgage may have grounds for foreclosing. The reasoning here is that if you reduce your equity level by taking out additional financing, the lender may be placed in a less secure position.

Due-on-Sale Clause: A clause in a mortgage specifying that the entire unpaid balance becomes due and payable on sale of the property. *See* Acceleration Clause.

Escrow Company: An independent third party (stakeholder) that handles funds; carries out the instructions of the lender, buyer, and seller in a transaction; and deals with all the documents. In most states, companies are licensed to handle escrows. In some parts of the country, particularly the Northeast, the function of the escrow company may be handled by an attorney.

FHA Loan: A mortgage insured by the Federal Housing Administration. In most cases, the FHA advances no money, but instead insures the loan to a lender such as a bank. There is a fee to the borrower, usually paid up front, for this insurance.

Fixed Rate Mortgage: A mortgage whose interest rate does not fluctuate for the life of the loan.

Fixer-Upper: A home that does not show well and is in bad shape. Often the property is euphemistically referred to in listings as a "TLC" (needs tender loving care) or "handy-man's special."

Foreclosure: Legal proceeding in which the lender takes possession and title to a property, usually after the borrower fails to make timely payments on a mortgage.

Fannie Mae: Any of the publicly traded securities collateralized by a pool of mortgages backed by the Federal National Mortgage Association. A secondary lender.

Freddie Mac: A publicly traded security collateralized by a pool of mortgages backed by the Federal Home Loan Mortgage Corporation. A secondary lender.

FSBO: For sale by owner.

Garbage Fees: Extra (and often unnecessary) charges tacked on when a buyer obtains a mortgage.

Graduated-Payment Mortgage: A mortgage whose payments vary over the life of the loan. They start out low, then slowly rise until, usually after a few years, they reach a plateau where they remain for the balance of the term. Such a mortgage is particularly useful when you want low initial payments. It is primarily used by first-time buyers, often in combination with a fixed rate or adjustable rate mortgage.

Growing Equity Mortgage: A rarely used mortgage whose payments increase according to a set schedule. The purpose is to pay additional money into principal and thus pay off the loan earlier and save interest charges.

HOA: Homeowners' Association, found mainly in condos but also in some single-family areas. It represents homeowners and establishes and maintains neighborhood architectural and other standards. You usually must get permission from the HOA to make significant external changes to your property.

Index: A measurement of an established interest rate used to determine the periodic adjustments for adjustable rate mortgages. There are a wide variety of indexes, including the Treasury bill rates and the cost of funds to lenders.

Inspection: A physical survey of the property to determine if there are any problems or defects.

Jumbo: A mortgage for more than the maximum amount of a Conforming Loan.

Lien: A claim for money against real estate. For example, if you had work done on your property and refused to pay the worker, he or she might file a "mechanic's lien" against your property. If you didn't pay taxes, the taxing agency might file a "tax lien." These liens "cloud" the title and usually prevent you from selling the property or refinancing it until they are cleared by paying off the debt.

Loan-to-Value Ratio (LTV): The percentage of the appraised value of a property that a lender will loan. For example, if your property appraises at $100,000 and the lender is willing to loan $80,000, the loan-to-value ratio is 80 percent.

Lock In: To tie up the interest rate for a mortgage in advance of actually getting it. For example, a buyer might "lock in" a mortgage at 7.5 percent so that if rates subsequently rose, he or she would still get that rate. Sometimes there's a fee for this. It's always a good idea to get it in writing from the lender, just to be sure that if rates rise the lender doesn't change its mind.

Low-Ball: To make a very low initial offer to purchase.

MAI: Member, American Institute of Real Estate Appraisers. An appraiser with this designation has completed rigorous training.

Margin: An amount, calculated in points, that a lender adds to an index to determine how much interest you will pay during a period for an adjustable rate mortgage. For example, the index may be at 7 percent and the margin, agreed upon at the time you obtain the mortgage, may be 2.7 points. The interest rate for that period, therefore, is 9.7 percent. *See also* Index, Points.

Median Sales Price: The midpoint of the price of homes—as many properties have sold above this price as have sold below it.

MLS: Multiple Listing Service—used by Realtors as a listings exchange. Nearly 90 percent of all homes listed in the country are found on the MLS.

Mortgage: A loan arrangement between a borrower, or "mortgagor," and a lender, or "mortgagee." If you don't make your payments on a mortgage, the lender can foreclose, or take ownership of the property, only by going to court. This court action can take a great deal of time, often six months or more. Further, even after the lender has taken back the property, you may have an "equity of redemption" that allows you to redeem the property for years afterward, by paying back the mortgage and the lender's costs. The length of time it takes to foreclose, the costs involved, and the equity of redemption make a mortgage much less desirable to lenders than a Trust Deed.

Mortgage Banker: A lender that specializes in offering mortgages but none of the other services normally provided by a bank.

Mortgage Broker: A company that specializes in providing "retail" mortgages to consumers. It usually represents many different lenders.

Motivated Seller: A seller who has a strong desire to sell. For example, the seller may have been transferred and must move quickly.

Multiple Counteroffers: Comeback offers extended by the seller to several buyers simultaneously.

Multiple Offers: Offers submitted simultaneously from several buyers for the same property.

Negative Amortization: A condition arising when the payment on an adjustable rate mortgage is not sufficiently large to cover the interest charged. The excess interest is then added to the principal, so that the amount borrowed actually increases. The amount that the principal can increase is usually limited to 125 percent of the original mortgage value. Any mortgage that includes payment Caps has the potential to be negatively amortized.

Origination Fee: An expense in obtaining a mortgage. Originally, it was a charge that lenders made for preparing and submitting a mortgage. The fee applied only to FHA and VA loans, which had to be submitted to the government for approval. With an FHA loan, the maximum origination fee was 1 percent.

Personal Property: Any property that does not go with the land. Such property includes automobiles, clothing, and most furniture. Some items such as appliances and floor and wall coverings are disputable. *See also* Real Property.

PITI: Principal, interest, taxes, and insurance. These are the major components that go into determining the monthly payment on a mortgage. (Other items include homeowner's dues and utilities.)

Points: A point is 1 percent of a mortgage amount, payable on obtaining the loan. For example, if your mortgage is $100,000 and you are required to pay 2½ points to get it, the charge to you is $2500. Some points may be tax deductible. Check with your accountant. A "basis point" is ¹⁄₁₀₀ of a point. For example, if you are charged ½ point (0.5 percent of the mortgage), the lender may refer to it as 50 basis points.

Preapproval: Formal approval for a mortgage from a lender. You have to submit a standard application and have a credit check. Also, the lender may require proof of income, employment, and money on deposit (to be used for the down payment and closing costs).

Prepayment Penalty: A charge demanded by the lender from the borrower for paying off a mortgage early. In times past (more than 25 years ago) nearly all mortgages carried prepayment penalties. However, those mortgages were also assumable by others. Today virtually no fixed rate mortgages (other than FHA or VA mortgages) are truly assumable, however some carry a prepayment penalty clause. *See* Assumption.

Private Mortgage Insurance (PMI): Insurance that protects the lender in the event that the borrower defaults on a mortgage. It is written by an independent third-party insurance company and typically covers only the first 20 percent of the lender's potential loss. PMI is normally required on any mortgage that exceeds an 80 percent loan-to-value ratio.

Purchase Money Mortgage: A mortgage obtained as part of the purchase price of a home (usually from the seller), as opposed to a mortgage obtained through refinancing. In some states, no deficiency judgment can be obtained against the borrower of a purchase money mortgage. (That is, if there is a foreclosure and the property brings less than the amount borrowed, the borrower cannot be held liable for the shortfall.)

Real Property: Real estate. This includes the land and anything appurtenant to it, including the house. Certain tests have been devised to determine whether an item is real property (goes with the land). For example, if curtains or drapes have been attached in such a way that they cannot be removed without damaging the home, they may be spoken of as real property. On the other hand, if they can easily be removed without damaging the home, they may be personal property. The purchase agreement should specify whether doubtful items are real or personal to avoid confusion later on.

Realtor®: A broker who is a member of the National Association of Realtors. Agents who are not members may not use the Realtor designation.

REO: Real estate owned—a term that refers to property taken back through foreclosure and held for sale by a lender.

RESPA: Real Estate Settlement Procedures Act. Legislation requiring lenders to provide borrowers with specified information on the cost of securing financing. Basically it means that before you proceed far along the path of getting the mortgage, the lender has to provide you with an estimate of costs. Then, before you sign the documents binding you to the mortgage, the lender has to provide you with a breakdown of the actual costs.

Second Mortgage: An inferior mortgage usually placed on the property after a first mortgage. In the event of foreclosure, the second mortgage is paid off only if and when the first mortgage had been fully paid. Many lenders will not offer second mortgages.

Short Sale: Property sale in which a lender agrees to accept less than the mortgage amount in order to facilitate the sale and avoid a foreclosure.

SREA: Society of Real Estate Appraisers—a professional association to which qualified appraisers can belong.

Subject To: A phrase often used to indicate that a buyer is not assuming the mortgage liability of a seller. For example, if the seller has an assumable loan and you (the buyer) "assume" the loan, you are taking over liability for payment. On the other hand, if you purchase "subject to" the mortgage, you do not assume liability for payment.

Subordination Clause: A clause in a mortgage document that keeps the mortgage subordinate to another mortgage.

Title: Legal evidence that you actually have the right of ownership of Real Property. It is given in the form of a deed (there are many different types of deeds) that specifies the kind of title you have (joint, common, or other).

Title Insurance Policy: An insurance policy that covers the title to a home. It may list the owner or the lender as beneficiary. The policy is issued by a title insurance company and specifies that if for any covered reason your title proves defective, the company will correct the title or compensate you up to a specified amount, usually the amount of the purchase price or the mortgage.

Trust Deed: A three-party lending arrangement that includes a borrower, or "trustor"; an independent third-party stakeholder, or "trustee" (usually a title insurance company); and a lender, or "beneficiary" so-called because the lender stands to benefit if the trustee turns the deed over in case the borrower fails to make payments. The advantage of the trust deed over the mortgage is that foreclosure can be accomplished without court action or deficiency judgment against the borrower. (In other words, if the property is worth less than the loan, the lender can't come back to the borrower after the sale for the difference.) *See also* Purchase Money Mortgage.

Upgrade: Any extra that a buyer may obtain when purchasing a new home—for example, a better-quality carpet or a wall mirror in the bedroom.

Upside Down: Owing more on a property than its market value.

VA Loan: A mortgage guaranteed by the Veterans Administration. The VA actually guarantees only a small percentage of the loan amount, but since it guarantees the "top" of the monies loaned, lenders are willing to accept the arrangement. In a VA loan the government advances no money; rather, the mortgage is made by a private lender such as a bank.

Wraparound Financing: A blend of two mortgages, often used by sellers to get a higher interest rate or facilitate a sale. For example, instead of giving a buyer a simple Second Mortgage, the seller may combine the balance due on an existing mortgage (usually an existing first) with an additional loan. Thus the wrap includes both the second and the first mortgages. The borrower makes payments to the seller, who then keeps part of the payment and in turn pays off the existing mortgage.

Resources

Once you make an offer and have it accepted, you will want to get a home inspection of the property. (Be sure your offer contains a clause stating that if you don't approve the inspection, you don't have to go through with the purchase and your deposit is to be returned!)

The big question becomes who shall you get to handle the inspection? One answer is to be sure the inspector is a member of a trade organization.

ASHI, American Society of Home Inspectors, is a national trade organization that encourages high standards for inspectors. Most important, it offers a written list of inspection criteria by which an inspector should judge your property. This list is quite extensive and helps provide for a more thorough inspection. You can contact ASHI to get a list of their members in your area from: *www.ashi.com.*

NAHI, National Association of Home Inspectors, is another national trade organization that also encourages high standards for its members. Ask if your inspector is a member. You can reach NAHI at: *www.nahi.com*

Additionally, you can ask your real estate agent to recommend an inspector. However, you should be aware that an agent could conceivably suggest an inspector who does a cursory examination so as to give a good report and quickly conclude a sale. Remember, your agent doesn't normally get paid until and unless the purchase is completed.

You can also check with your state department of real estate. Go on the Web and look for your state government offices. You'll quickly find the real estate division—all states have them. Keep in mind, however, that home inspectors are *not*, as this point, licensed or regulated in most states. Nevertheless, some real estate departments will offer guidelines for finding good inspectors in their state.

There are local also trade organizations for home inspectors in many states. You can learn about these through ASHI, NAHI, the state department of real estate, or by checking with several local inspectors.

Finally, be aware that typically the inspection report will contain a host of disclaimers including the fact that the inspector is not liable for any areas he or she cannot see (such as under carpets). For that reason you may wish to additionally make your own home inspection. To help you with this you may want to read my books, *Tips & Traps When Renovating Your Home,* McGraw-Hill, 1999, and *The Home Inspection Trouble-Shooter,* Dearborn, 1995.

Index

About the Author

Robert Irwin, one of America's leading experts in all areas of real estate, is the author of more than 40 books, including McGraw-Hill's best-selling Tips and Traps series. For more real-estate tips and traps, go to www.robertirwin.com.